HARCOURT ART EVERYWHERE

AUTHORS

Jacqueline Chanda

Kristen Pederson Marstaller

CONSULTANTS

Katherina Danko-McGhee

María Teresa García-Pedroche

Harcourt

SCHOOL PUBLISHERS

Orlando   Austin   New York   San Diego   Toronto   London

Visit *The Learning Site!*

www.harcourtschool.com

Dear Young Artist,

In this book, you will be introduced to artists and artworks from around the world and across the centuries. You will learn what the smallest sketch and the largest sculpture have in common—the elements of art and the principles of design that can be found in all artworks.

Artists use the elements and principles to try to capture the look and the feel of the world as they see it. Their thoughts and ideas become preserved in artworks that viewers can enjoy.

As you learn about art in this book, you will create artworks of your own, just as artists have done for thousands of years. Your drawings, paintings, and sculptures will capture the look and the feel of the world as *you* see it.

Sincerely,

The Authors

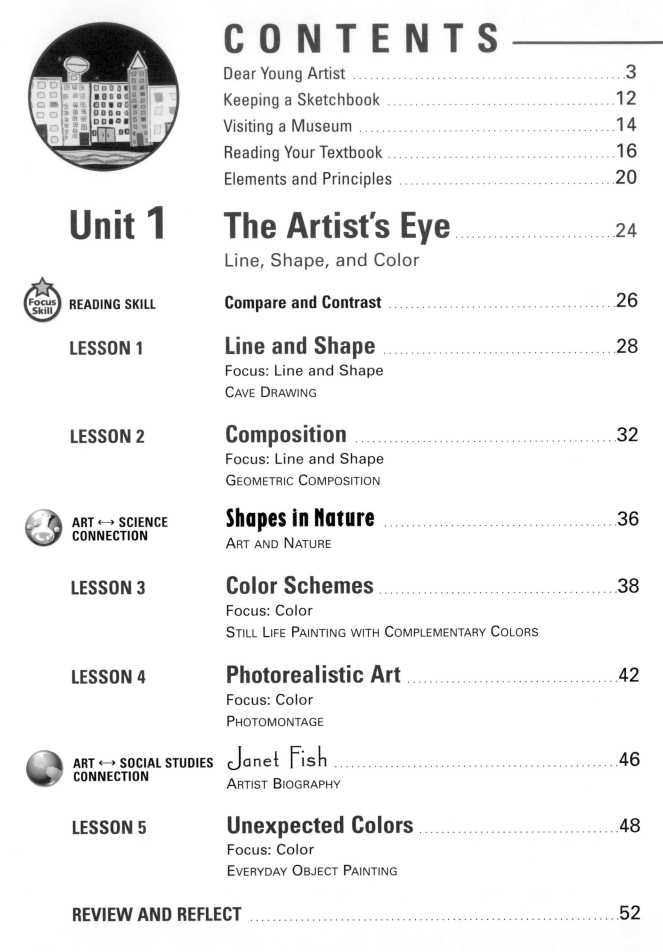

CONTENTS

Unit 3 Journey into Art 84

Space, Emphasis, and Movement

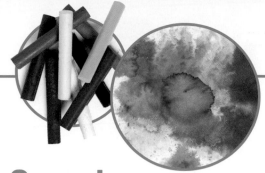

AT A GLANCE

Art Production

Elements and Principles

Cross-Curricular Connections

Media

Keeping a
Sketchbook

When you make sketches and keep them together, you are keeping an art sketchbook. You can carry your sketchbook with you. Use it to make notes about your ideas, to sketch things you see, or to sketch what you imagine.

The artist M. C. Escher imagined patterns made up of shapes that fit together perfectly.

▲ M. C. Escher,
Self-Portrait.

In this sketch, Escher figured out how to make the heads and tails of fish fit together like the pieces of a puzzle. He often wrote notes and dates on his sketches. He used some of the sketches to create finished paintings.

M. C. Escher, ▶
Symmetry #20.

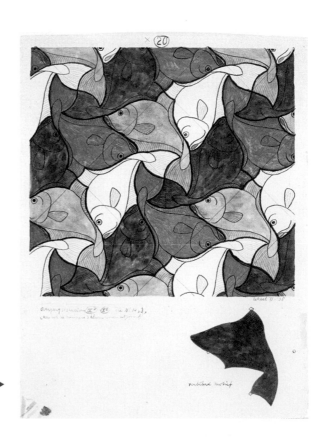

Using a sketchbook is a good way to plan a finished artwork. You can sketch the composition of a painting, rearrange the parts of a sculpture, or experiment with patterns in a design. You can also practice your drawing skills.

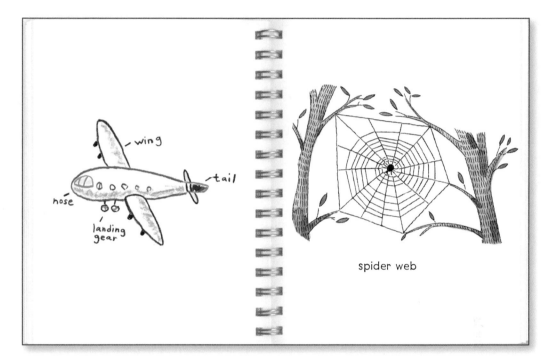

spider web

You may want to collect poems, pictures, and textures that interest you. You can tape or glue them into your sketchbook. These things may give you ideas for art projects. If you write notes and dates next to your entries, your sketchbook will be a valuable resource for many years to come.

Runners, Summer

Visiting a
Museum

An art museum is a place where artworks are collected and displayed. You can find art museums in cities and towns all over the world.

When you visit an art museum, remember to

- **Walk** slowly through the museum. Pause at the artworks that catch your eye. Read the information about them.

- **Look** closely at the artworks, but don't touch them.

- **Think** about what each artist's message might be.

- **Listen** carefully to what the docent or guide tells you about the artworks.

- **Speak** quietly, but don't be afraid to ask questions.

▲ **The George Washington Carver Museum**
Tuskegee, Alabama

◀ **The Metropolitan Museum of Art**
New York, New York

 Fast Fact The Met, as it is called, is one of the largest art museums in the United States. It contains more than two million objects.

Looking at Art

You may see artworks in museums, in books, or on websites. When you look at an artwork, you can follow these steps to better understand what you see:

- **DESCRIBE**   Look closely at the artwork, and tell what you see. How would you describe the artwork to someone who has not seen it?

- **ANALYZE**   Look at the way the artist organized the parts of the artwork. What part of it catches your eye first?

- **INTERPRET**   Think about the idea or feeling the artist may be expressing in the artwork. Sometimes the title of an artwork can help you understand the artist's message.

- **EVALUATE**   Use your observations about the artwork to form an opinion of it. Do you think the artist was successful?

◀ The San Antonio Art League Gallery & Museum

San Antonio, Texas

Fast Fact *The Art League Museum takes its name from the group of local artists who first exhibited their works in San Antonio in 1894.*

Reading Your Textbook

Knowing how to read your art textbook will help you remember and enjoy what you read. Each lesson contains nonfiction text about artists, artworks, art techniques, and art history. Remember that nonfiction texts give facts about real people, things, events, or places.

The title tells the main topic of the lesson.

You can identify the most important ideas in each lesson by becoming familiar with the different features of your textbook. Look at this sample lesson from pages 42–45.

Highlighted words are art vocabulary.

Lesson 4

Vocabulary
representational
photorealistic
photomontage

Photorealistic Art

Subjects in **representational** art look real, or realistic. In most ways, they look like real people, places, and things. Some representational painters ignore the details of their subjects, making them look less real. **Photorealistic** painters copy every detail they see. Their paintings might be mistaken for photographs.

Photographic Paintings
Look at image . Does it look more like a painting or a photograph? Photographic images contain bright reflections and dark shadows. Describe the reflections and shadows in image A. Objects in photographs have clear lines and sharp edges. Describe the lines and edges of the objects in image A.

 John Baeder,
White Rose System,
1993, oil on canvas,
$24\frac{1}{4}$ in. × $36\frac{1}{4}$ in.
O. K. Harris Art Gallery,
New York, New York.

42

Captions next to each artwork give information such as the artist's name and the title of the artwork. Captions may also provide information about an artwork's date, materials, dimensions, and location. Subheads can provide clues about the ideas found in different sections of a lesson.

B Steve Vidler, *66 Diner, Albuquerque, New Mexico,* photograph.

"Painterly" Photographs

The dramatic color scheme in the photograph in image **B** makes it look like a painting. Are the edges of the objects in this photograph clear and sharp, or soft and blurry?

Painters can carefully choose and place colors on a canvas, but photographers must find real color schemes in real settings. Look closely at the color scheme in image **B**. Which two colors stand out? Name this kind of color scheme.

Captions give important information about each artwork.

Subheads signal the beginning of a new section of text.

43

Reading Your Textbook

Other features of your textbook link artworks to related subject areas. Questions at the end of each lesson help you think about what you have learned.

Links give facts related to an artist or an artwork.

Think Critically questions assess what you have learned.

This logo 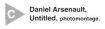 shows a good place to use your reading skills.

Social Studies Link

In 1826 a French inventor named Joseph Nicéphore Niépce (nee•say•FAWR nyehps) coated a metal plate with a light-sensitive chemical and exposed it to light, using a primitive camera. The picture, showing the view from Niépce's window, was the world's first photograph.

Daniel Arsenault, **Untitled**, photomontage.

Photomontages

Photographs are the materials that an artist uses to create a **photomontage**. Look at the photomontage in image C. Some of the photographs have been cut into different sizes and shapes. How are the subjects of the photographs alike? How would you describe the theme of this photomontage?

Think Critically

1. **READING SKILL** Compare and contrast the shadows in images A and B. **COMPARE AND CONTRAST**

2. List some of the details that make the building in image A look as real as it would look in a photograph.

3. **WRITE** Imagine the town that surrounds the building in image A. Describe its location and size. Describe the people who live there.

44

You can find more resources in the Student Handbook:

- Maps of Museums and Art Sites, pp. 206–209
- Art Safety, pp. 210–211
- Art Techniques, pp. 212–227
- Elements and Principles, pp. 228–239
- Gallery of Artists, pp. 240–253
- Glossary, pp. 254–261
- Art History Time Line, pp. 262–263

Artist's Workshop

Make a Photomontage

MATERIALS
- magazines
- scissors
- poster board
- glue

PLAN

Choose a color scheme for a photomontage. Look through magazines and other sources to find photographs that contain the colors in your color scheme. You may want to choose photographs related to a theme, such as school, home, or community.

CREATE

1. Cut the photographs that you find into various sizes, and sort the pieces by color.

2. Arrange the pieces loosely on a sheet of poster board. Rearrange them to find the most interesting composition of colors and shapes.

3. Glue the pieces to the poster board.

REFLECT

Describe the color scheme you used. Explain why you arranged the photographs the way you did.

 Safety Tips Remember to point sharp objects away from your body.

Artist's Workshop activities are organized by the steps Plan, Create, and Reflect.

Photographs show how an artwork can be made.

Tips provide information about art techniques or safety.

45

Elements of Art

The **elements of art** are the basic parts of an artwork. You can use them to describe art and to create your own artworks. As you look at these photographs, think about other places where you have seen the elements of art.

SHAPE ▲

an object that has height and width

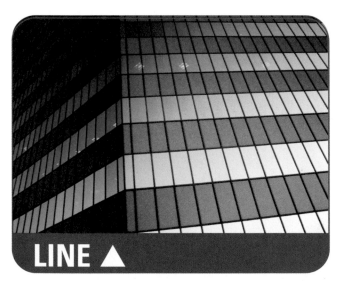

LINE ▲

a mark that begins at one point and continues for a certain distance

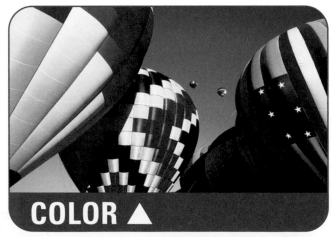

COLOR ▲

what we see when light is reflected off objects

See also Elements and Principles, pages 228–239.

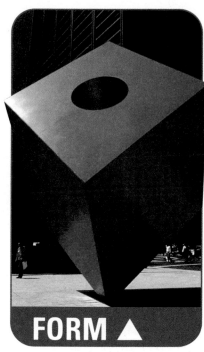

FORM ▲

an object that has height, width, and depth

SPACE ▲

the area around, between, or within objects

TEXTURE ▲

the way a surface looks or feels

VALUE ▲

the lightness or darkness of a color

21

Principles of Design

Artists use the **principles of design** to arrange art elements in artworks. As you look at these photographs, notice how the arrangement of elements affects you.

BALANCE ▲

the steady feeling created by the equal weight of elements on both sides of an artwork

PATTERN ▲

a recognizable design made with repeated lines, shapes, or colors

PROPORTION ▲

a sense that objects are the correct size in comparison to each other

VARIETY ▲

the interesting effect created when one element is different from other elements in an artwork

See also Elements and Principles, pages 228–239.

EMPHASIS ▲

the effect created when one element is given more importance than another element

RHYTHM ▲

the visual beat created by the regular repetition of elements in an artwork

MOVEMENT ▲

the way the viewer's eyes travel from one element to another in an artwork

UNITY ▲

the sense that an artwork is complete and that its parts work together as a whole

Edouard Manet, *Claude Monet and His Wife in His Floating Studio,*
1874, oil on canvas, 80 cm × 98 cm.

LOCATE IT

This painting can be found at the Neue Pinakothek
(NOY•uh peen•ah•koh•TEK), a museum in Munich,
Germany.

See Maps of Museums and Art Sites, pages 206–209.

GERMANY

Munich

The Artist's Eye

Step into the Art

Imagine that you could enter the painting *Claude Monet and His Wife in His Floating Studio*. What would it feel like to step aboard the boat? What sights, smells, and sounds of the river would greet you? What would you say to the artist and his wife, and what might they reply?

ABOUT THE ARTIST

See Gallery of Artists, pages 240–253.

Unit Vocabulary

gesture drawing

contour lines

geometric shapes

organic shapes

composition

abstract art

expressive qualities

nonobjective

monochromatic

value

analogous colors

complementary colors

representational

photorealistic

photomontage

Surrealism

hue

saturation

Pop Art

Multimedia Art Glossary
Visit *The Learning Site*
www.harcourtschool.com

Compare and Contrast

**When you think about how things are alike, you *compare*.
When you think about how things are different, you *contrast*.
Look at the images below.**

This is how they are alike:

- Images **A** and **B** are both colorful artworks.

- Images **A** and **B** both have pieces of fruit as the subject.

This is how they are different:

- Image **A** is a painting, but image **B** is a sculpture.

- Image **A** creates a feeling of calmness, but image **B** creates a feeling of excitement.

A **Paul Cézanne,**
The Basket of Apples,
about 1895, oil on canvas, 65 cm × 80 cm.
Art Institute of Chicago, Chicago, Illinois.

B **Claes Oldenburg, *Dropped Bowl
with Scattered Slices and Peels,***
1990, steel, concrete, plastic, enamel,
16 ft. 9 in. × 91 ft. × 105 ft. Metro Dade
Open Space Park, Miami, Florida.

Comparing and contrasting can help you understand what you see and what you read. Read this passage about Paul Cézanne (say•ZAHN) and Claes Oldenburg (KLAHS OHL•duhn•burg). Think about how the artists are alike and different.

Paul Cézanne was a famous French artist who often painted food, flowers, and everyday items such as baskets and pottery. He painted these objects just as he saw them.

Claes Oldenburg is a Swedish American artist whose sculptures show food and common objects in a giant size. He helps viewers see familiar objects in a new and interesting way.

Compare and contrast Paul Cézanne and Claes Oldenburg. Use this diagram to help you.

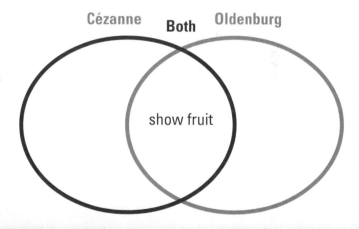

Cézanne Both Oldenburg

show fruit

On Your Own

As you read the lessons in this unit, use Venn diagrams like the one above to compare and contrast information that you read and artworks that you see. Look back at your diagrams when you see questions with **Focus Skill** *READING SKILL* .

Line and Shape

From ancient times to modern times, artists have used lines and shapes to record their experiences. Look at the ancient cave drawing in image **A**, and describe what you see. What shapes did the artist use to show horses and sheep? Now look at the modern drawing in image **B**. The artist used loose arm movements, or gestures, to create this rough **gesture drawing**. Compare the lines and shapes in image **A** with those in image **B**. How are they alike and different?

 Unknown artist, *Men on Horseback with Mountain Sheep,* Native American Ute culture, about 1680 to 1880, pigment on rock face, about 3 ft. × 3 ft. Arches National Park near Moab, Utah.

 Pablo Picasso, *Don Quixote,* 1955, pen and ink. Musée d'Art et d'Histoire, St. Denis, France.

Characteristics of Lines

When you describe the characteristics of a line, you describe the way it looks. Lines may be straight or curved, wavy or zigzag, thick or thin. What are the characteristics of the lines in the ancient cave painting in image C? The artist used **contour lines**, or outlines, to draw a chief's face. Describe the characteristics of those contour lines. The lines below the face suggest a royal costume. What are the characteristics of those lines?

 Unknown artist,
Four Faces Panel (detail),
about A.D. 400 to 1300, pigment
on rock. Canyonlands, Utah.

Kinds of Shapes

Compare the ancient artwork in image C with the modern painting in image D. How are the two artworks alike and different? Look for **geometric shapes**, such as circles, triangles, and squares, in both paintings. Natural shapes, like those of leaves and petals, are called **organic shapes**. Point out the organic shapes in images C and D.

 Paul Klee, *The Black Prince,*
1927, oil, 13 in. × 11.4 in. Kunstsammlung
Nordrhein-Westfahlen, Dusseldorf, Germany.

29

Unknown artist,
The Red Horse and the Bull,
13,000 B.C., pigment on rock face. Lascaux Caves II, Lascaux, France.

Social Studies Link

The Lascaux Grotto, a cave in southern France, was discovered by four teenage boys on a hike in 1940. The boys entered the cave through a hole made by a fallen tree, and found prehistoric art on the cave walls.

Cave Paintings

What is the subject of image E? What are the characteristics of the lines the artist used? Describe the kinds of shapes you see in image E.

Ancient cave paintings have been found all over the world. Many appear to be gesture drawings sketched with charcoal and then finished with red or brown paint. Artists today use charcoal made of charred branches, just as artists did thousands of years ago.

Think Critically

1. **Focus Skill** **READING SKILL** Compare and contrast the cave art in image A and in image E. COMPARE AND CONTRAST

2. Describe at least two ways in which ancient artists were like artists today.

3. **WRITE** Imagine you could use only a few lines and shapes to draw a family member. What lines and shapes would you use, and why would you use them?

Artist's Workshop

Make a Cave Drawing

MATERIALS

- sketchbook
- pencil
- tan-colored construction paper
- crayons
- black poster board
- glue

PLAN

Imagine you are a cave painter in ancient times. What plants and animals would you include in a cave painting? Make several sketches in your sketchbook.

CREATE

1. Copy your best sketch onto tan-colored construction paper. Use black crayon to outline objects. Make some lines thick and some lines thin.

2. Use dark reds, browns, and other earth-colored crayons to finish your drawing.

3. Crumple the paper and straighten it out. Do this several times. Then glue your drawing onto black poster board.

REFLECT

Point out the different kinds of lines and shapes you used. Tell why you chose certain colors for certain objects.

Quick Tip

Be careful not to tear your paper as you crumple it. Smooth it out gently before you crumple it again.

31

Composition

When artists arrange, or put together, objects in an artwork, they create a **composition**. Some artists rearrange the parts of objects to create unusual compositions.

Abstract Compositions

Look at image **A**. How would you describe it? Image **A** is an example of **abstract art**. Abstract artists distort or simplify parts of real objects and rearrange them in unusual ways. Describe how the artist of image **A** simplified the parts of the musicians' bodies. What kind of shapes did he use for the musical instruments?

Describe the appearance, or characteristics, of the lines in image **A**. Lines can also have **expressive qualities** that create a mood or a feeling. What feeling do you get from the lines in image **A**? What kind of music do you imagine the musicians are playing?

 Gil Mayers,
Arrangement II,
1998, mixed media.
Private collection.

In image **B** the artist used a computer to create an abstract artwork of a city. Compare and contrast the buildings in this artwork with buildings in a real city. How are they alike and different?

Describe the characteristics of the lines in image **B**. What are the expressive qualities of those lines? What mood or feeling do they create?

B Diana Ong, *Monopoly*, 2001, computer graphics. Collection of the artist.

Photographic Compositions

Photographers look through the lenses of their cameras to find interesting compositions in the world around them.

C *Tel Aviv, Israel,* photograph.

Look at image **C**. The photographer looked at part of a building and found an interesting arrangement of lines and shapes. What kinds of lines do you see in this photograph? Identify the geometric shapes you see.

Nonobjective Compositions

Some abstract artworks are not meant to show any real people, places, or things. These artworks are called **nonobjective** because they don't show objects. Look at image D. How would you describe it? How did the artist of image D use lines and shapes in interesting ways? What feeling do you think the artist was trying to express when she created this artwork?

 Maria, age 10, Untitled.

Think Critically

1. **READING SKILL** Compare and contrast the shapes in image C and image D. COMPARE AND CONTRAST

2. Look for an interesting arrangement of lines and shapes in a small section of your classroom. Tell why it would make an interesting photograph.

3. **WRITE** Describe the lines you would use to draw a special place. Include both the lines' characteristics and their expressive qualities.

Artist's Workshop

Create a Geometric Composition

MATERIALS

- geometric objects
- white paper
- pencil
- colored markers

PLAN

Think of ways you can arrange geometric shapes in a nonobjective artwork. Collect objects that you can trace to draw squares, rectangles, triangles, and circles.

CREATE

1. Trace your objects on white paper. Draw enough shapes to fill the page.

2. Add straight, zigzag, or wavy lines to your composition of shapes.

3. Use markers to color your artwork.

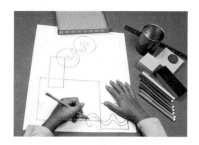

REFLECT

Describe the lines and shapes you used. Explain why you placed them where you did.

 Quick Tip

Trace the same objects several times in different areas of your design.

35

Shapes in Nature

Can shapes in nature look like abstract art?

Have you ever noticed the shape of an icicle or the wavy lines in tree bark? The lines and shapes we see in nature often look like abstract art. With scientific tools, we can look very closely at natural objects to see interesting compositions of lines and shapes.

Image **A** shows a diamond as seen through the lens of a powerful microscope. Image **B** shows a piece of lettuce through the same type of lens. Compare and contrast these images with abstract artworks you have seen.

Microscope photograph of a diamond, Molecular Expressions Photo Gallery.

Microscope photograph of lettuce tissue, Molecular Expressions Photo Gallery.

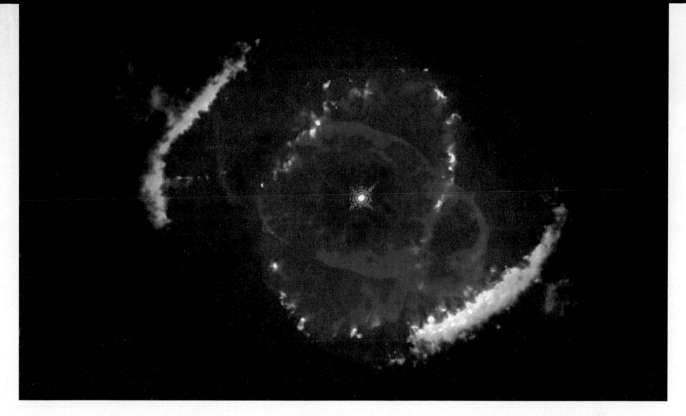

Hubble Space Telescope photograph of a dying star, HubbleSite News Center Archive.

Image **C** shows a huge object in outer space seen through a powerful space telescope. A scientist might describe image **C** as a picture of a star reaching its final stage. How might an artist describe image **C**?

Think About Art

Look closely at a familiar object. Imagine what it would look like through the lens of a powerful microscope. What geometric or organic shapes do you think you would see?

DID YOU KNOW?

American artist Georgia O'Keeffe was inspired by the lines and shapes of nature throughout her life. What lines and shapes did she use in *Shell #1*?

Georgia O'Keeffe, *Shell #1*, 1928, oil on canvas, 17.8 cm x 17.8 cm. National Gallery of Art, Washington, D.C.

37

Vocabulary

monochromatic

value

analogous colors

complementary
colors

Color Schemes

Artists carefully plan which colors they will use in their artworks. They select a group of colors, or a color scheme, for each work.

Monochromatic Color Schemes

A **monochromatic** color scheme includes one color and the lighter and darker versions of that color. The darkness or lightness of a color is its **value**.

Look at the monochromatic painting in image . Notice the pure blue color in the skirt of the kneeling girl. The artist added black to this color to create the darker values, or shades, of blue in the painting. He added white to create the lighter values, or tints, of blue.

The color chart below shows values of blue. See if you can find these tints and shades in image .

Color Values

tints   shades

Henry O. Tanner,
Moses in the Bullrushes,
1921, oil on wood, 22$\frac{3}{8}$ in. × 15$\frac{1}{4}$ in.
Smithsonian American Art Museum,
Washington, D.C.

Cool Colors, Warm Colors

Artists may use a color wheel like the one at the right to plan a color scheme. One kind of color scheme might include all the warm colors, from yellow through red-violet. Which colors would you choose to create a cool-color scheme?

Analogous Color Schemes

Colors that are next to each other on the color wheel are called **analogous colors**. Analogous colors—such as green, yellow-green, and blue-green—fit well together because they have at least one color in common. What color do they all contain? In image **B** the artist used an analogous color scheme. Which analogous colors did he choose?

LOCATE IT

The painting in image **B** can be found at the San Antonio Art League Museum.

TEXAS

San Antonio

See Maps of Museums and Art Sites, pages 206–209.

 Ralph White, *Galveston*,
1949, oil on masonite, 22 in. × 32 in.
San Antonio Art League Museum,
San Antonio, Texas.

Louis Valtat,
Bouquet of Flowers,
oil on canvas, 18$\frac{1}{4}$ in. × 15 in.

Complementary Color Schemes

Colors that are far apart on the color wheel create a bold color contrast when placed side by side. **Complementary colors**, such as yellow and violet, are opposite each other on the color wheel. Which complementary color pair do you see in image C? Look back at the color wheel on page 39. Find two more pairs of complementary colors.

Think Critically

1. **READING SKILL** Compare and contrast the color schemes used in image A and image C. **COMPARE AND CONTRAST**

2. What kind of feeling do you get from image B? How would your feeling be different if the artist had used a warm color scheme?

3. **WRITE** Write sentences that compare and contrast images B and C. Use a Venn diagram to organize your ideas.

Artist's Workshop

Paint a Still Life with Complementary Colors

MATERIALS

- group of objects
- white poster board
- pencil
- tempera paints
- paper plate
- water cup
- paintbrush

PLAN

Your teacher will set up a group of objects for a still-life painting. Look back at the color wheel on page 39, and choose a pair of complementary colors for your still life.

CREATE

1. Sketch your still life on white poster board. Decide where you will use each complementary color.

2. Mix tints and shades of the first complementary color, and paint those areas.

3. Rinse your paintbrush. Mix tints and shades of the second complementary color, and paint those areas.

REFLECT

Explain why you chose certain colors for certain parts of your painting. Point out how you used value.

Quick Tip

You may choose a third color for some of the details in your painting. Paint those areas last.

Photorealistic Art

Subjects in **representational** art look real, or realistic. In most ways, they look like real people, places, and things. Some representational painters ignore the details of their subjects, making them look less real. **Photorealistic** painters copy every detail they see. Their paintings might be mistaken for photographs.

Photographic Paintings

Look at image . Does it look more like a painting or a photograph? Photographic images contain bright reflections and dark shadows. Describe the reflections and shadows in image A. Objects in photographs have clear lines and sharp edges. Describe the lines and edges of the objects in image A.

A John Baeder,
White Rose System,
1993, oil on canvas,
$24\frac{1}{4}$ in. × $36\frac{1}{4}$ in.
O. K. Harris Art Gallery,
New York, New York.

Steve Vidler, *66 Diner, Albuquerque, New Mexico,*
photograph.

"Painterly" Photographs

The dramatic color scheme in the photograph in image **B** makes it look like a painting. Are the edges of the objects in this photograph clear and sharp, or soft and blurry?

Painters can carefully choose and place colors on a canvas, but photographers must find real color schemes in real settings. Look closely at the color scheme in image **B**. Which two colors stand out? Name this kind of color scheme.

In 1826 a French inventor named Joseph Nicéphore Niépce (nee•say•FAWR nyehps) coated a metal plate with a light-sensitive chemical and exposed it to light, using a primitive camera. The picture, showing the view from Niépce's window, was the world's first photograph.

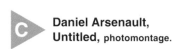
Daniel Arsenault, **Untitled,** photomontage.

Photomontages

Photographs are the materials that an artist uses to create a **photomontage**. Look at the photomontage in image C. Some of the photographs have been cut into different sizes and shapes. How are the subjects of the photographs alike? How would you describe the theme of this photomontage?

Think Critically

1. **READING SKILL** Compare and contrast the shadows in images A and B. COMPARE AND CONTRAST

2. List some of the details that make the building in image A look as real as it would look in a photograph.

3. **WRITE** Imagine the town that surrounds the building in image A. Describe its location and size. Describe the people who live there.

Artist's Workshop

Make a Photomontage

MATERIALS

- magazines
- scissors
- poster board
- glue

PLAN

Choose a color scheme for a photomontage. Look through magazines and other sources to find photographs that contain the colors in your color scheme. You may want to choose photographs related to a theme, such as school, home, or community.

CREATE

1. Cut the photographs that you find into various sizes, and sort the pieces by color.

2. Arrange the pieces loosely on a sheet of poster board. Rearrange them to find the most interesting composition of colors and shapes.

3. Glue the pieces to the poster board.

REFLECT

Describe the color scheme you used. Explain why you arranged the photographs the way you did.

Safety Tips

Remember to point sharp objects away from your body.

Janet Fish

How does an artist capture sunlight on a canvas?

Janet Fish was born in Boston, Massachusetts, but she grew up on the sunny island of Bermuda. She studied art at a time when most artists were painting in an abstract style. Janet Fish, however, wanted to paint real objects exactly as she saw them. She developed a realistic style overflowing with sunlight and color, as in image **A**.

 Janet Fish, *Green Glass from Alexis,*
2001, oil on canvas, 50 in. x 70 in.
Harn Museum, Gainesville, Florida.

Most of Janet Fish's paintings include ordinary glass pieces, such as vases, plates, and windows, that seem to glow and sparkle with energy. Point out the tints and shades she used to show light and shadows in images **A** and **B**.

Janet Fish often paints objects given to her by friends. Her work includes titles such as *Green Glass from Alexis*, *Hunt's Vase*, and *Ilka's Teapot*. She gives objects to her friends, too. A pair of her candlesticks or a glass vase from her own kitchen may appear in another artist's still life.

DID YOU KNOW?

A transparent object lets light travel through it without bending or scattering the light. That is why you can see through a glass object to its other side.

Think About Art

Look at the glass pieces in Janet Fish's paintings. How did the artist show that these pieces are see-through, or transparent?

GO ONLINE **Multimedia Art Biographies**
Visit *The Learning Site*
www.harcourtschool.com

Unexpected Colors

Sometimes artists use unrealistic colors in realistic paintings. Artists are always free to change the colors of real people, places, and things. When they do, viewers may feel surprised.

Shocking Colors

Look at image **A**, and describe what you see. Why do you think the artist painted his subject that color? Image **A** is an example of **Surrealism**, a type of art that includes fantastic or dreamlike images. Artists who paint in this style may use color in unexpected ways to shock the viewer.

The man in image **A** has been painted in a pure **hue**, or unmixed color. Pure colors have high **saturation**, or brightness. Hues are brighter than tints, shades, or other mixed colors. What could you do to lower the saturation of the blue in the man's figure in image **A**? Where in image **A** did the artist use tints and shades of blue? Compare the saturation of the tints and shades with the saturation of the pure blue in the man's figure.

 Andre Rouillard, *The Blue Man,*
acrylic on canvas, 24 in. × 16 in.
Private collection, Mortagne, France.

Image **B** shows a realistic portrait of a dog painted with unrealistic colors. Why do you think the artist used this color scheme? Point out areas of high saturation on the dog. Where did the artist use tints and shades of blue?

Describe the saturation of the background color in image **B**. Notice the strong color contrast between the blue dog and the bright yellow background. Does this contrast create a calm feeling or an excited feeling?

 Gabby L., age 10,
My Blue Dog,
acrylic.

Playful Colors

Image **C** is an example of **Pop Art**. Pop artists often choose unusual colors for ordinary objects. This gives viewers a fresh look at familiar things. Describe the color scheme of each soup can shown in image **C**. What colors are used on the real labels of this familiar soup?

Andy Warhol,
Campbell's Soup Cans,
1965, silkscreen on canvas,
four canvases, each 36 in. × 24 in.
Private collection.

LOCATE IT

Many of Andy Warhol's artworks can be found at the Andy Warhol Museum in Pittsburgh, Pennsylvania.

PENNSYLVANIA

Pittsburgh

See Maps of Museums and Art Sites, pages 206–209.

Think Critically

1. **READING SKILL** Compare and contrast the color schemes of the soup cans in image **C**. Which do you like best, and why? **COMPARE AND CONTRAST**

2. Think of a familiar object. If you were painting it in the Pop Art style, how would you change its colors?

3. **WRITE** Choose a new color scheme for image **A**. Write a paragraph describing the color scheme and explaining why you would use it.

Artist's Workshop

Paint an Everyday Object

MATERIALS

- everyday object
- white paper
- pencil
- watercolors
- water cup
- paintbrush

PLAN

Find a familiar object to paint a picture of. Choose an object with a simple shape, such as a soccer ball, a backpack, or a favorite food.

CREATE

1. Fold your paper lengthwise and width-wise to create four equal sections. Sketch your object in each of the four sections.

2. Plan a different color scheme for each section. Remember that the background color is an important part of each color scheme.

3. Use watercolors to paint each section.

REFLECT

Explain why you chose your color schemes.

Quick Tip

Let each section dry completely before you paint the next one.

Unit 1 Review and Reflect

Choose the letter of the word or phrase that best completes each sentence.

1 Circles, squares, and triangles are examples of ___ shapes.

    A organic   **C** value

    B gesture   **D** geometric

2 Artists arrange objects and shapes into ___.

    F values   **H** squares

    G compositions   **J** circles

3 Colors located next to each other on the color wheel are called ___ colors.

    A monochromatic   **C** analogous

    B complementary   **D** value

4 Photorealistic painters create artworks that look like ___.

    F statues   **H** shapes

    G photographs   **J** Pop Art

5 A color that has high saturation is ___.

    A pale   **C** bright

    B monochromatic   **D** dull

READING SKILL

Compare and Contrast

Select two artworks from this unit, and reread the information about them. Use a Venn diagram to compare and contrast the information about each artwork.

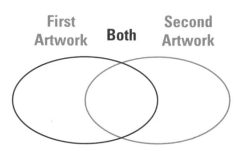

First Artwork   Both   Second Artwork

Write About Art

Choose two pieces of your own artwork. Write two paragraphs in which you compare and contrast them. Use a Venn diagram to plan your writing. Use unit vocabulary words to describe each artwork.

REMEMBER — YOU SHOULD

- write about the similarities in one paragraph and the differences in the other.

- use correct grammar, spelling, and punctuation.

Critic's Corner

Look at *New Orleans: Ragging Home* by Romare Bearden to answer the questions below.

Romare Bearden,
New Orleans: Ragging Home,
1974, collage with acrylic and lacquer on board, $36\frac{1}{8}$ in. × 48 in. North Carolina Museum of Art, Raleigh, North Carolina.

DESCRIBE How would you describe what is happening in the artwork?

ANALYZE What shapes do you see in the artwork? Where did the artist use contour lines? Where did the artist use analogous colors?

INTERPRET What feeling do you think the artist wanted to express?

EVALUATE Do you think the artist successfully expressed a feeling or created a mood? Explain your answer.

Robert Glen, *The Mustangs of Las Colinas,*
1984, nine bronze statues and pool, 354 ft. × 60 ft. × 10 ft.

LOCATE IT

This sculpture can be found in Williams Square, Irving, Texas.

See Maps of Museums and Art Sites, pages 206–209.

Irving

TEXAS

Putting It Together

Step into the Art

How would you describe the horses in *The Mustangs of Las Colinas*? Why do you think they might be running? Where do you think they might be going? If you could stand near them, what sounds might you hear?

ABOUT THE ARTIST

See Gallery of Artists, pages 240–253.

Unit Vocabulary

patterns	overlapping	construction
grid	tessellation	assemblage
motif	two-dimensional	found objects
still life	three-dimensional	open form
positive shape		closed form
negative shape	positive space	geometric forms
	negative space	organic forms

Multimedia Art Glossary
Visit *The Learning Site*
www.harcourtschool.com

Author's Purpose

An author has a purpose for writing—such as to inform, to influence, to express, or to entertain. An artist has a purpose for creating an artwork, too.

Look at the painting in image **A**, and read its title. Describe what is happening in this scene. Which details in the painting show that the man is teaching the boy to play the banjo? The artist's purpose may have been to inform the viewer about the way skills are passed down from one musician to another.

A Henry O. Tanner, *The Banjo Lesson,* 1893, oil on canvas, 49 in. × 35½ in. Hampton University Museum, Hampton, Virginia.

Read this passage about Henry O. Tanner's life. Then think about the author's purpose for writing it. Do you think the author wanted to inform, to influence, to express, or to entertain?

The American artist Henry O. Tanner was born in Pittsburgh, Pennsylvania, in 1859. His father was a bishop in the African Methodist Episcopal Church. Due to his father's influence, many of Tanner's paintings show scenes from the Bible.

Tanner received his early art training in Philadelphia, Pennsylvania. Then, in 1891, he traveled to Paris, France. He lived and worked there until his death in 1937.

Use this diagram to list some details from the passage. Decide whether the author would use these details to inform, to influence, to express, or to entertain.

Author's/Artist's Purpose		
Detail	Detail	Detail
born in 1859		

On Your Own

As you read the lessons in this unit, use charts like the one on this page to help you determine the purpose of the text you read and of the artworks you see. Look back at your charts when you see questions with **Focus Skill** *READING SKILL* .

Patterns in Paintings

Artists repeat lines, shapes, and colors in their artworks to create **patterns**. Some artists imagine new and unusual patterns, while others paint the patterns they see around them.

Grid Patterns

Look at the artwork in image **A**. How would you describe the patterns the artist created? What repeating lines, shapes, and colors do you see? Notice the way the shapes are lined up in horizontal rows and vertical columns. When rows and columns cross, they form a **grid** like the pattern on graph paper. If the artist had added another row or column to image **A**, what do you think it would look like?

 Marilee Whitehouse-Holm,
Abstract #4,
gouache and oil pastel
on paper, 16 in. × 22 in.
Private collection.

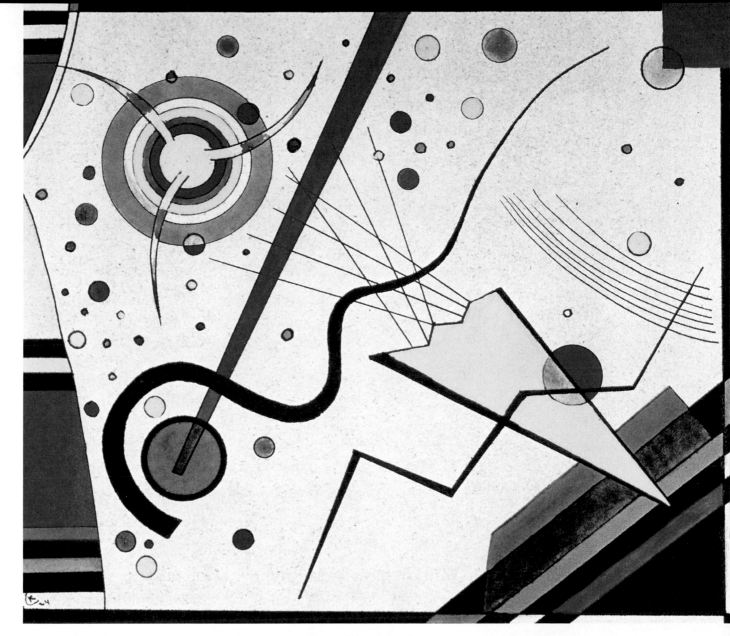

Wassily Kandinsky,
Variation VI,
1924, ink and watercolor.
Bauhaus Archive, Tiergarten,
Berlin, Germany.

Motifs

In image B, the artist used patterns in certain areas of
the artwork. Find the stripes of color in image B. In this
artwork, stripes are a **motif**. Motifs are repeated lines, shapes,
or objects that help organize a composition. Which stripes in
image B are horizontal? Which are diagonal? Where did the
artist repeat stripes in a circle? Look for another motif in
image B.

LOCATE IT

Image C can be found in the Musée d'Orsay (moo•ZAY dawr•SAY) in Paris, France.

See Maps of Museums and Art Sites, pages 206–209.

Realistic Patterns

Artists often include realistic patterns in paintings, such as the **still life** in image C. Long ago a still life always included objects that were once alive, such as fruit or flowers. Today the term *still life* applies to any painting whose subject is a group of objects.

Notice the way the artist of image C arranged the fruit into groups. Count the pieces of fruit in front of the pitcher. Now count the pieces of fruit in the tall bowl. How did the artist use the fruit to create a pattern?

Think Critically

1. **READING SKILL** What do you think the artist's purpose was for the painting in image B—to inform, to influence, to express, or to entertain? **AUTHOR'S/ARTIST'S PURPOSE**

2. Imagine that image B is a scene in outer space. What objects might the shapes represent?

3. **WRITE** Describe what the fruit in image C would feel, smell, and taste like. Use at least three sentences.

 Paul Cézanne, *Apples and Oranges*, about 1895–1900, oil on canvas, 29$\frac{1}{8}$ in. × 36$\frac{5}{8}$ in. Musée d'Orsay, Paris, France.

Artist's Workshop

Paint a Still Life with Patterns

MATERIALS

- small classroom objects
- white paper
- pencil
- watercolors
- paintbrush
- water bowl

PLAN

Collect groups of similar objects, such as boxes, balls, and cans. Arrange the objects on a table. Create a pattern by grouping similar objects together.

CREATE

1. Sketch your arrangement on white paper.

2. Choose colors for your objects that will help create additional patterns.

3. Use watercolors to paint your still life.

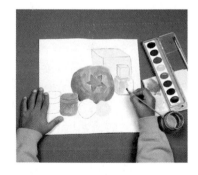

REFLECT

Point out where you created patterns. Describe the colors, shapes, and lines you used to create each pattern.

Quick Tip

You may want to share objects with a group of classmates so that you will have more choices.

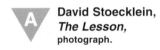
Positive and Negative Shapes

Each subject in a painting or a photograph has a shape. Point out one of the subjects in image **A**. The shape of a subject is a **positive shape**. The shape of the empty space around a subject is a **negative shape**. Positive and negative shapes fit together like puzzle pieces.

Positive and Negative Patterns

Look at the pattern of positive shapes in image **A**. Trace with your finger the pattern of negative shapes between the cowboys. Positive shapes overlap when part of one shape covers part of another shape. Where are the **overlapping** shapes in this photograph?

▼ **A** David Stoecklein,
The Lesson,
photograph.

Tessellations

The fish shapes in image **B** fit together perfectly without overlapping. They form a pattern called a **tessellation**. In a tessellation, subjects have no empty space around them. Can you find any negative shapes in image **B**?

Look back at image **A**. Notice how the cowboys seem closer to the viewer than the empty areas around them do. Now look at image **B**. Which fish seem closer to the viewer? If you look closely at one color of fish, those fish seem to be closest to you. Looking closely at one group of shapes in a tessellation makes them appear to be positive shapes.

LOCATE IT

The artwork in image C can be found at the Lowe Art Museum in Miami, Florida.

See Maps of Museums and Art Sites, pages 206–209.

Some artists use geometric shapes to make tessellations like the one in image **C**. Name the geometric shapes you see in this artwork. Notice how they tessellate, or fit together, without overlapping and without leaving spaces between them. Do the shapes shown below tessellate?

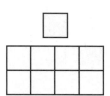

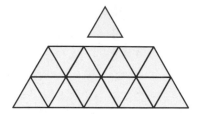

Explain why the shapes shown here do not tessellate.

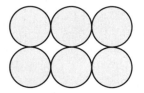

 Roy Lichtenstein,
Modular Painting in Four Panels,
1969, oil on canvas, 108 in. × 108 in.
The Lowe Art Museum, Miami, Florida.

Think Critically

1. **READING SKILL** Do you think the artist of image **B** wanted to inform, to influence, to express, or to entertain?
   AUTHOR'S/ARTIST'S PURPOSE

2. Look around your classroom. Identify the positive and negative shapes you see. Can you find any tessellations?

3. **WRITE** Cowboys are the photographer's subject in image **A**. If you were a photographer, what subject would you like to photograph? Explain your answer.

Artist's Workshop

Create a Tessellation

MATERIALS

- graph paper
- ruler
- pencil
- markers

PLAN

Think of ways you could create a tessellation using geometric shapes. Remember that in a tessellation, none of the shapes overlap and there are no spaces between shapes.

CREATE

1. Use a ruler to draw diagonal lines through the squares on a piece of graph paper.

2. Outline the shapes that are part of your tessellation.

3. Choose a color scheme, and then use markers to color the shapes of your tessellation.

REFLECT

Point out where you repeated shapes and colors to create patterns.

Quick Tip

Color the partial shapes at the edges of your tessellation so there are no white spaces left.

M.C. ESCHER

Is it possible to draw the impossible?

M. C. Escher (ESH•er) was born in the Netherlands in 1898. For the first half of his life, he made a living by drawing nature scenes, such as waterfalls and forests. Then he took a trip that changed the direction of his artwork completely.

Escher sailed to Spain, where he became fascinated by the tessellations, or interlocking geometric patterns, on the buildings that he saw. From that day on, Escher began to include geometric puzzles, tricks of the eye, and impossible worlds in his art.

Look at the interlocking hands in image **A**. The drawing seems to be creating itself! In image **B**, squares in a field turn into birds in the air. Where do the white birds and the black birds fit together like puzzle pieces?

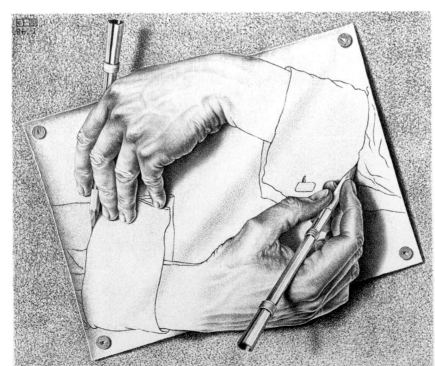

M. C. Escher,
Drawing Hands,
1948, lithograph,
$11\frac{1}{8}$ in. x $13\frac{1}{8}$ in.

M. C. Escher,
Day and Night,
1938, lithograph.

Image shows a sketch for a tessellation. Notice how Escher designed the fish's tail. Where in image C do four tails fit together?

For many years, mathematicians were the greatest admirers of Escher's work. Then in 1959, a collection of his art was published, and Escher found admirers among art fans, too. Today millions of people all over the world admire his one-of-a-kind patterns, puzzles, and impossibilities.

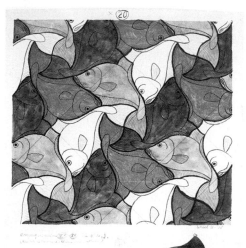

C   **M. C. Escher,**
Symmetry #20,
lithograph.

Think About Art

Find shapes in image **B** that could be either positive or negative.

Multimedia Biographies
Visit *The Learning Site*
www.harcourtschool.com

DID YOU KNOW?

The Alhambra is a fortress and palace in southern Spain. M. C. Escher was inspired by the colorful, interlocking patterns that cover many of its floors, walls, and ceilings.

Vocabulary

two-dimensional

three-dimensional

positive space

negative space

construction

Patterns in Sculpture

Paintings are flat, **two-dimensional** artworks that have two measurements—height and width. Sculptures are **three-dimensional** artworks that have height, width, and depth.

Look at the wooden sculpture in image . The artist painted a pattern of shapes on its surface. What do you think these shapes represent? Where are the patterns in the sculpture in image ?

 Unknown artist,
Monument to Progress in Transportation,
Cleveland, Ohio.

 Unknown artist, *Northwest Native American sculpture,* nineteenth century, wood.

Positive and Negative Spaces

A raised area in a sculpture is a **positive space**. A lower area is a **negative space**. Point out the positive and negative spaces in the statue in image **B**. Describe the patterns you see.

Now look at the granite sculpture in image **C**. Where are the positive and negative spaces? This artwork is an example of a **construction**, a sculpture built from separate pieces of similar material. Describe the pattern you see in image **C**. Why do you think the artist calls this sculpture a "granite weaving"?

 Jesús Moroles, *Texas Shield*, 1986, granite, $97\frac{3}{4}$ in. × 45 in. × $44\frac{1}{2}$ in. Modern Art Museum, Fort Worth, Texas.

Social Studies Link

The sculpture in image D comes from the Ivory Coast, a country in Africa. It was used for measuring gold powder.

AFRICA

Ivory Coast

Casting Sculptures

The artwork in image D is made of brass—a combination of copper and zinc. It was made by a process called casting. In casting, a metal or other substance is heated until it melts. The liquid metal is poured into a mold, or cast. After the metal cools and hardens, the object is removed from the cast.

Describe the pattern of positive and negative spaces in the artwork in image D. Point out the spaces that have organic shapes. Which spaces have geometric shapes?

 D Unknown artist, **Geometric figurine,** brass. Musée des Arts d'Afrique et d'Oceanic, Paris, France.

Think Critically

1. **Focus Skill** *READING SKILL* Images B and C both show monuments. Why do you think the artists created them? AUTHOR'S/ARTIST'S PURPOSE

2. Examine several types of coins. Identify the positive spaces and the negative spaces on them.

3. **WRITE** Which method of sculpting would you like to try—carving, construction, or casting? Explain your answer.

Artist's Workshop

Carve a Clay Tile

MATERIALS

- sketchbook
- pencil
- clay slab
- craft stick
- paper clip
- bowl of water

PLAN

Draw a large rectangle in your sketchbook. Then draw a pattern of organic and geometric shapes inside the rectangle.

CREATE

1. Refer to your sketch as a guide. Use a pencil point to lightly carve your pattern into the surface of a slab of clay.

2. Use a craft stick or paper clip to remove the clay and create the negative spaces in your pattern.

3. Dip your fingers in water, and smooth any rough edges in your design. Allow the clay slab to dry.

REFLECT

Point out the positive and negative spaces in your tile. Describe the techniques you used to create the tile.

Safety Tips

Remember to point the sharp objects you are working with away from your body.

71

Lesson
9

Vocabulary

assemblage

found objects

open form

closed form

Surprising Sculptures

Some artists combine different kinds of materials in one artwork. This kind of sculpture is called an **assemblage**. Some assemblages are made by arranging various objects into larger forms. Look at the sculptures in images **A** and **B**. Do they look like any sculptures you have seen before?

Assemblages with Found Objects

Most objects are made for a purpose. When an artist uses them for a different purpose in an artwork, they are called **found objects**. Some artists use natural objects, such as dried flowers, stones, or seashells, in their assemblages. Others use manufactured objects, such as machine parts, toys, or tools. Point out the found objects in image **A**. What was their original purpose? What kind of pattern did the artist create with found objects?

A **Nam June Paik,** *Technology,*
1991, video monitors, laser disc players, and cabinet, 127 in. × 51$\frac{7}{8}$ in. × 75$\frac{5}{8}$ in. Smithsonian American Art Museum, Washington, D.C.

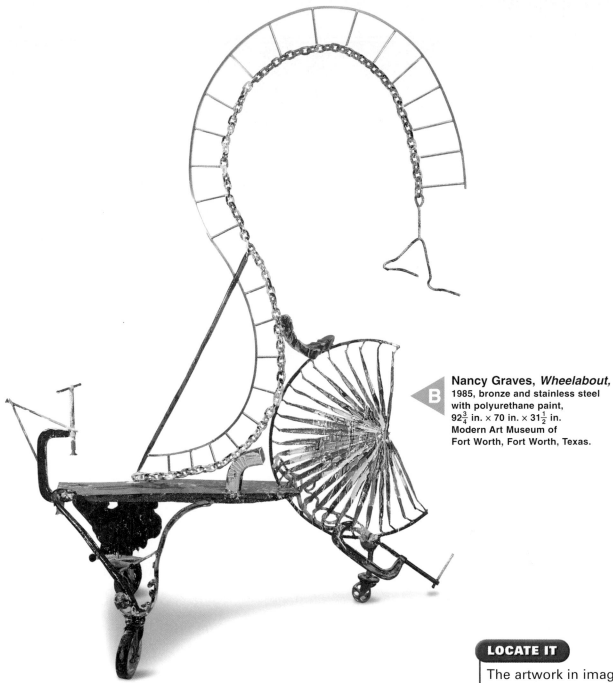

B Nancy Graves, *Wheelabout,*
1985, bronze and stainless steel
with polyurethane paint,
$92\frac{3}{4}$ in. × 70 in. × $31\frac{1}{2}$ in.
Modern Art Museum of
Fort Worth, Fort Worth, Texas.

LOCATE IT

The artwork in image
B can be found at the
Modern Art Museum
of Fort Worth, in Fort
Worth, Texas.

See Maps of Museums
and Art Sites,
pages 206–209.

Open-Form Sculptures

Describe the different objects that make up the sculpture in
image B. Which objects do you think the artist built especially
for this artwork? Which objects do you think the artist found?

The sculpture in image B is an **open form**. Open-form
sculptures have openings where background space shows
through. Point out the open spaces you see in image B. Where
did the artist create a pattern by repeating the shapes of open
spaces?

Closed-Form Sculptures

The artwork in image **C** is a **closed form**. Closed-form sculptures have no openings where background space shows through. For the assemblage in image **C**, the artist arranged images and objects in a solid box. What do you think the theme of this artwork is?

Think Critically

1. **READING SKILL** Why do you think the artist created the assemblage in image **C**? AUTHOR'S/ARTIST'S PURPOSE
2. Look at objects in your classroom. Which objects would you like to use in a found-object assemblage?
3. **WRITE** Imagine that image **C** showed objects from the artist's life. Write a paragraph about the objects and the artist.

Artist's Workshop

Make a Memory-Box Assemblage

MATERIALS

- shoebox lid
- acrylic paints
- paintbrush
- small personal objects
- glue

PLAN

Gather objects that are important to you, such as photographs and small toys. You may want to choose objects related to a theme, such as *school, family,* or *community.*

CREATE

1. Paint your box lid. Choose a color that matches one of the colors in your objects.

2. After the paint has dried, move the objects around in the box lid until you find the best arrangement.

3. Glue your objects into the box lid.

REFLECT

Describe the different shapes and forms in your assemblage. Explain why the objects in your assemblage are important to you.

Quick Tip

You may want to include small natural objects, such as seashells or dried flowers, in your assemblage.

SCULPTING MOUNT RUSHMORE

How could a sculptor carve faces that are more than 60 feet high?

When sculptor Gutzon Borglum (GUHT•suhn BAWR•gluhm) looked at the blank face of Mount Rushmore, he imagined huge sculpted portraits of four United States Presidents.

To make his dream a reality, Borglum first created small models in his studio. Image **A** shows one of his models, with the uncarved Mount Rushmore in the background. He then made the larger model shown in image **B**. The finished portraits were to be twelve times the size of the larger model. The measuring device shown in image **C** allowed Borglum to take precise measurements of the faces in the larger model. He then multiplied them by twelve, and applied them to the faces on the mountain.

 B Gutzon Borglum with larger model of Mount Rushmore statues

 A Gutzon Borglum at work in his studio

C Device used by Borglum to measure models of Mount Rushmore statues

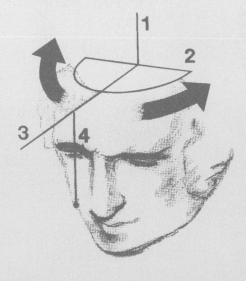

The sculpting of Mount Rushmore took fourteen years, from 1927 to 1941. More than 500,000 tons of rock had to be removed from the mountain by a small crew of workers who used explosives and heavy equipment. Few had any artistic training at all. Most were miners. Yet they created an astounding work of art that is still the largest sculpture in the world.

THINK ABOUT ART

If you could carve a gigantic sculpture on the face of a mountain, what would you sculpt? Why?

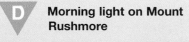

Multimedia Biographies
Visit *The Learning Site*
www.harcourtschool.com

▽ **Morning light on Mount Rushmore**

Functional Forms

Look around your classroom. You are sitting inside a geometric form. **Geometric forms** have length, width, and depth. Each side, or wall, of a geometric form is a geometric shape. Architects combine geometric forms, or rooms, when they build schools, houses, or other buildings.

Forms for Living

Look at the geometric forms below. Identify the forms that are part of the house shown in image A.

Geometric Forms

cube

square pyramid

rectangular prism

 A Claude Monet,
La Maison Weue,
Zaandau,
1871, oil on canvas,
114.3 cm × 153.7 cm.
Private collection.

World-famous architect Frank Lloyd Wright added round geometric forms to his house designs. Look at the forms below, and then point out the cylinder and cone in the house shown in image **B**.

Geometric Forms

cylinder   cone

B Frank Lloyd Wright, *Walter Gale House,* 1892. Oak Park, Illinois.

Organic Forms

The imaginary house in image **C** is made up of **organic forms**. The sides of organic forms have irregular shapes. Describe the forms you see in the house in image **C**.

C Bishara, age 10, *House of Creativity.*

79

LOCATE IT

The building in image
D is located in Vienna,
Austria. Austria is a
country in western
Europe.

Vienna

AUSTRIA

See Maps of Museums
and Art Sites,
pages 206–209.

The real apartment building in image **D** is also made up of organic forms. Its walls, floors, and ceilings have irregular shapes. Would you rather live in this building or in the one shown in image **A**? Explain your answer.

Friedrich
Hundertwasser,
Hundertwasser House,
1986.

Think Critically

1. **READING SKILL** Why do you think an architect might design a building like the one in image **D**? AUTHOR'S/ARTIST'S PURPOSE

2. Describe what it might be like to live in the house in image **C**.

3. **WRITE** Write a paragraph to describe your dream house. Name some of the shapes and forms it would have.

Artist's Workshop

Paint Your Dream House

- white paper
- pencil
- watercolors
- paintbrush
- water bowl
- black marker

PLAN

Imagine a dream house that is made of several different forms such as cones, cylinders, pyramids, and cubes.

CREATE

1. Draw your dream house on white paper.

2. Use watercolors to paint the sections of your house.

3. Use a black marker to add details to the house, such as shutters, railings, a pattern on the roof, or fancy trim.

REFLECT

Point out the forms that make up your dream house.

Quick Tip

You may want to look in magazines to find pictures of houses with interesting forms and details.

Unit 2 Review and Reflect

Vocabulary and Concepts

Choose the letter of the word or phrase that best completes each sentence.

1 Artists repeat lines, shapes, or colors to create ___.

   A space   **C** patterns

   B tints   **D** shades

2 A still life is an artwork that shows a group of ___.

   F people   **H** animals

   G objects   **J** buildings

3 A sculpture can have positive and negative ___.

   A prints   **C** colors

   B motifs   **D** spaces

4 A sculpture made from different kinds of materials is called ___.

   F a portrait   **H** a figure

   G an assemblage **J** a grid

5 Cubes and pyramids are examples of ___.

   A lines   **C** shapes

   B spaces   **D** forms

 **READING SKILL**

Author's Purpose

Reread the first paragraph on page 77. Use a chart like this one to list details from the text. Then decide whether the author wanted to inform, to influence, to express, or to entertain.

Author's/Artist's Purpose		
Detail	Detail	Detail

Write About Art

Choose a classmate's artwork from this unit. Write a paragraph describing the artist's purpose for creating the artwork. Use a chart to help you list details about the work. Then decide whether the artist wanted to inform, to influence, to express, or to entertain.

REMEMBER — YOU SHOULD

■ include details that will help readers understand the artist's purpose.

■ use correct grammar, spelling, and punctuation.

Critic's Corner

Look at the vase at the right to answer these questions.

DESCRIBE What patterns do you see in this artwork?

ANALYZE How might people use this object?

INTERPRET Why do you think the artist created this object?

EVALUATE Do you think the artist achieved his or her purpose? Explain your answer.

Unknown artist,
Antique Chinese Vase,
porcelain.

83

Julian Onderdonk, *A Cloudy Day, Bluebonnets near San Antonio, Texas,* 1918, oil on canvas, $25\frac{1}{8}$ in. × $30\frac{1}{8}$ in.

LOCATE IT

This painting can be found at the Amon Carter Museum in Fort Worth, Texas.

See Maps of Museums and Art Sites, pages 206–209.

TEXAS

Fort Worth

Journey into Art

Step into the Art

Imagine that you could enter the field of flowers shown in the painting. Would you walk through the field, or would you run? Would you sit down to enjoy the flowers? Describe the sights, sounds, and smells that would surround you.

ABOUT THE ARTIST

See Gallery of Artists, pages 240–253.

Unit Vocabulary

point of view	proportion	linear perspective
emphasis	placement	vanishing point
space	movement	environmental art
horizon line	atmospheric perspective	installation
perspective	diffusion	

Multimedia Art Glossary
Visit *The Learning Site*
www.harcourtschool.com

Main Idea and Details

The *main idea* tells what something is mostly about. *Details* provide information to explain and support the main idea.

Look at the image below. The main idea of the painting is the beauty of the harvest season. You may find clues about an artwork's main idea in its title. Then you can look for details, which support the main idea:

- the activities of the people in the painting

- the equipment in the painting

- the golden glow of the fields

Vincent van Gogh, *The Harvest at La Crau,*
1888, oil on canvas, 73 cm × 92 cm. Van Gogh Museum, Amsterdam.

Read this passage about the artist Vincent van Gogh (van GOH) and his work. Think about the main idea of the passage and the details that support it.

Vincent van Gogh loved to paint nature scenes. He carefully studied nature and the changes in the seasons. His favorite season to paint was summer, when nature was in full bloom. He tried to capture the bright blue sky and the golden fields of summer on his canvas. In July of 1888, Vincent van Gogh painted ten nature scenes in only ten days.

Find the main idea in the passage, and write it in a diagram like this one. Fill in the other boxes with details that support the main idea.

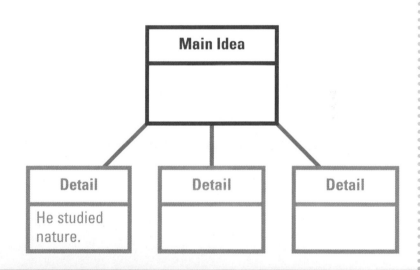

Main Idea		
Detail	**Detail**	**Detail**
He studied nature.		

On Your Own

As you read the lessons in this unit, use diagrams like the one above to find the main idea and the supporting details in the text that you read and in the artworks that you see. Look back at your diagrams when you see questions with **Focus Skill** *READING SKILL* .

Artist's Point of View

When you look at a painting, think about where the artist was sitting or standing while creating the artwork. This is the artist's **point of view**. Imagine yourself painting the scene in image **A**. Are you sitting or standing? Find the people in the scene who are sitting closest to you. Is your eye level above their heads? How can you tell?

Now look at image **B**. Do you think the artist was standing or sitting while creating this artwork? The subjects closest to the artist have **emphasis**, or importance, in image **B**. If the artist of image **A** had been sitting, how would that painting be different? Which people would be emphasized?

▼
A

Martha Walter, ***Blustery Day at the Beach,*** 1925, oil on board, 14 in. × 18 in. David David Gallery, Philadelphia, Pennsylvania.

Camille Pissarro,
Haymakers Resting,
1891, oil on canvas,
$25\frac{3}{4}$ in. × 32 in. McNay
Art Museum, San
Antonio, Texas.

Space in Landscapes

The element of **space** is the empty area between, around or within objects. The space that is shown in a painting is divided into the foreground, the middle ground, and the background. The objects that appear closest to the viewer are in the foreground. The objects that appear farthest from the viewer are in the background. The space between the foreground and the background is called the middle ground.

Point to the background in image **A**. Find the line where the land and sea seem to meet the sky. This is the **horizon line**. When a viewer stands on flat ground and looks straight ahead, the horizon line stretches across the center of his or her view. Is the horizon line in image **A** high, low, or in the center of the painting? Compare the horizon lines in image **A** and image **B**. Why do you think the horizon line is higher in image **B**?

LOCATE IT

The painting in image
C can be found at the
Smithsonian American
Art Museum in
Washington, D.C.

Washington, D.C.

See Maps of Museums
and Art Sites,
pages 206–209.

Dedrick Brandes Stuber,
Passing Clouds, 1933–34,
oil on canvas, $40\frac{1}{8}$ in. × 50 in.
Smithsonian American Art
Museum, Washington, D.C.

Bird's-Eye View

Imagine yourself as the painter of the scene in image C. Find
the rooftop in the foreground of the painting. What does it tell
you about your point of view? Where does the horizon line
appear when the viewer looks straight ahead from a high point
of view? Which objects in the background did the artist want
to emphasize? Look at the title of the painting for a clue.

Think Critically

1. **READING SKILL** Identify the main idea and at least two
   supporting details in image A. **MAIN IDEA AND DETAILS**

2. Describe what image B would look like if the artist had
   painted the women from a bird's-eye point of view.

3. **WRITE** Imagine you are looking down on your
   classroom from above. Describe what you see.

Artist's Workshop

Draw from Two Different Points of View

MATERIALS

- white paper
- pencil
- colored pencils

PLAN

Think of a beach or another place where you can see the horizon line. Imagine what the place would look like from a low point of view and from a high point of view.

CREATE

1. Draw a vertical line down the center of your paper. On the left side, sketch the horizon line where it would appear if you were sitting on the ground.

2. On the right side, sketch the horizon line where it would appear if you were looking out from a tall building.

3. Add objects to your scene. Use colored pencils to complete your drawing.

REFLECT

Explain why the same objects look different when seen from a low point of view and from a high point of view.

Quick Tip

Sketch lightly so that black pencil lines will not show through the colors of your finished drawing.

Depth and Perspective

Artists use the technique of **perspective** to create a feeling of depth, or distance, in their paintings. Perspective is a way of making some objects seem close to the viewer and others seem farther away.

Proportion and Placement

One way artists apply perspective to their paintings is by using the principle of proportion. **Proportion** is the size of one object in comparison to another.

Look at image **A**. Compare the sizes of the people in the foreground, middle ground, and background. Figures that are farther from the artist are shown smaller. This difference in size creates a sense of depth in the painting.

Now look at the **placement**, or position, of the people in the foreground, middle ground, and background. Figures that are farther from the artist are placed higher up than those that are closer to the artist. Placing figures in this way creates a sense of depth in the painting.

 Pierre-Auguste Renoir, *Ball at the Moulin de la Galette* (detail), 1876, oil on canvas, 175 cm × 131 cm. Musée d'Orsay, Paris, France.

Movement

An artist guides the **movement** of the viewer's eyes from place to place in an artwork. In image the artist used color and size to emphasize the largest sailboat, making it the viewer's starting point. The viewer's eyes move next to the smaller boats, and then to the horizon line. Finally, the viewer's eyes move to the bright waves in the foreground. Where do you think the artist was standing or sitting when he created this painting? How did he use proportion and placement to create a sense of distance?

B Vincent van Gogh,
Fishing Boats at Saintes-Marie-de-la-Mer,
1888, oil on canvas, 44 cm × 53 cm. Pushkin Museum of Fine Arts, Moscow, Russia.

What part of the painting in image C do you notice first? How did the artist use size and color to draw your attention to this part first? What do you notice next? Describe how your eyes move around the painting.

How did the artist use proportion and placement to create a feeling of depth in this painting?

Think Critically

1. **(Focus Skill) READING SKILL** What is the main idea in image C? Which details in the painting help make the main idea clear? **MAIN IDEA AND DETAILS**

2. Describe the movement your eyes take around the painting in image A.

3. **WRITE** Think of your favorite outdoor place. Describe the people, animals, or objects you would include in a painting of your favorite place.

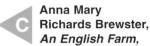
Anna Mary Richards Brewster, *An English Farm,* 1899, oil on canvas, 20 in. × 16 in. The Louise and Alan Sellars Collection of Art by American Women, Indianapolis, Indiana.

Artist's Workshop

Paint an Outdoor Scene

MATERIALS

- white paper
- pencil
- watercolors
- paintbrush
- paper plate
- water cup

PLAN

Imagine an outdoor scene that includes people, animals, and objects.

CREATE

1. Sketch a person, animal, and object in the foreground, in the middle ground, and in the background.

2. To make figures and objects look farther away, draw them smaller and higher on the paper.

3. Paint your scene.

REFLECT

Explain how you used size and placement to create a sense of distance in your painting.

Quick Tip

Before you paint, look at the copying master that has a diagram of size and placement.

GEORGE WASHINGTON CARVER

Can a scientist also be an artist?

George Washington Carver was one of the most famous scientists and inventors ever born in the United States.

Two United States Presidents, Calvin Coolidge and Franklin Roosevelt, traveled to Carver's laboratories in Tuskegee, Alabama, to show their respect for him. The great inventor Thomas Edison wanted Carver to move north and work for him, but Carver refused to go. In his long career, Carver found hundreds of uses for crops grown in Alabama and other southern states.

Carver was also a talented artist who carefully observed nature. As a child, he was always drawing and labeling the plants near his home in Missouri. He showed great promise as a young painter. Image shows one of his oil paintings. Two of his artworks were judged good enough to be shown at the Chicago World's Fair in 1893.

A **George Washington Carver**, *Still Life*, oil on linen, 133 cm x 68.5 cm., Tuskegee Institute National Historic Site, Tuskegee, Alabama.

Carver continued to draw and paint throughout his life, and he never stopped inventing. He even invented a process for making his own paint. Image **B** shows the results of one of his experiments. The frame on the right includes a small landscape painting by Carver.

In 1941 Carver's friend and fellow inventor Henry Ford traveled to Tuskegee to dedicate the George Washington Carver Museum. The museum was built to house papers, experiments, and artworks from all of Carver's life. The great scientist, inventor, and artist died two years later. Many of his paintings were destroyed by fire just six years after that, but most of his scientific experiments survived.

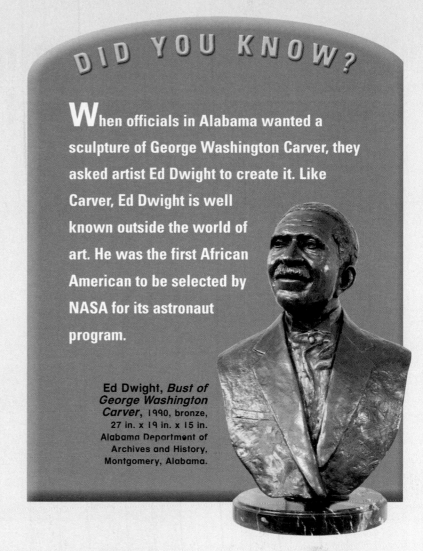

DID YOU KNOW?

When officials in Alabama wanted a sculpture of George Washington Carver, they asked artist Ed Dwight to create it. Like Carver, Ed Dwight is well known outside the world of art. He was the first African American to be selected by NASA for its astronaut program.

Ed Dwight, *Bust of George Washington Carver*, 1990, bronze, 27 in. x 19 in. x 15 in. Alabama Department of Archives and History, Montgomery, Alabama.

 Paint sample with miniature landscape, 36 cm x 12.8 cm.

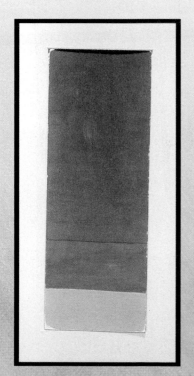

THINK ABOUT ART

What skills do artists and scientists have in common?

Multimedia Biographies
Visit *The Learning Site*
www.harcourtschool.com

Vocabulary

atmospheric
  perspective

diffusion

Atmospheric Perspective

The painting in image **A**, *Mona Lisa* by Leonardo da Vinci (dah VIN•chee), is one of the first examples of a technique called **atmospheric perspective**. Artists apply this technique by blurring the details of objects that are farthest from them. What do you notice about the objects in the background of image **A**?

Leonardo da Vinci,
Mona Lisa,
about 1503–06, oil on
wood, 77 cm × 53 cm.
Musée du Louvre, Paris,
France.

B Unknown artist,
*Emigrant Party on
the Road to California*,
1850, lithograph, $4\frac{3}{0}$ in. $\times$ $6\frac{7}{8}$ in.
Newberry Library, Chicago,
Illinois.

Space and Distance

Have you ever looked at a distant mountain range or a city
skyline? At some point in the distance, objects begin to look
blurry. Water, dust, or smoke in the air creates **diffusion**, or
the scattering of light. This makes details look less crisp.
Look at the scene in image . Where do the edges of the
people and objects start to look fuzzy?

Warm colors are difficult to see when you look into
the distance, but blues and purples remain clear. Point out
the warm colors in image B. At what point in the scene do
the warm colors disappear? What colors do you see in the
background of the scene?

C Emiliano di Cavalcanti, *Headland*, 1926, oil on canvas.

Look for examples of atmospheric perspective in image C. Where do the details begin to look blurry? Where do you see warm colors? What colors are clearest in the background?

Think Critically

1. **READING SKILL** What is the main idea in image B? What details support this main idea? **MAIN IDEA AND DETAILS**

2. How did the artist of image B use proportion to create a sense of depth?

3. **WRITE** Look at the most distant parts of the scenes in images A, B, and C. Describe what they have in common.

Artist's Workshop

Paint a Mountain Landscape

MATERIALS

- **white paper**
- **pencil**
- **watercolors**
- **paintbrush**
- **paper plate**
- **water cup**

PLAN

Imagine an outdoor scene with mountains on the horizon line. Think about ways you can use atmospheric perspective to paint this scene.

CREATE

1. Sketch your scene on white paper.

2. Paint objects in the foreground first, using bright colors. Mix duller colors, and use them to paint the middle ground.

3. Use purples and blues to paint the background. Lightly brush water over the mountains to blur the edges.

REFLECT

Describe the colors you used in the foreground, middle ground, and background. Explain how you used them to create a sense of distance in your painting.

Quick Tip

To make a color duller, add some of its complement.

101

Linear Perspective

Imagine that you are standing outdoors, looking down a long road. Does the road seem to get wider or narrower in the distance? The parallel lines on the sides of a road seem to converge, or come closer together, in the distance. Artists create this sense of distance in their artworks by using a technique called **linear perspective**.

Look at the lines on each side of the ceiling in image **A**. They appear to be closer to each other at the far end of the kitchen because they extend back, away from the viewer. Now look at the lines that form the kitchen window. The lines of the window do not appear to converge because they do not extend away from the viewer. What other objects in image **A** have lines that do not converge?

 John Lawrence Groff,
Kitchen,
1989, oil on canvas,
28 in. × 22 in. Private
collection, Amherst,
Massachusetts.

LOCATE IT

The painting in image **B** can be found at the Art Institute of Chicago in Chicago, Illinois.

Chicago

ILLINOIS

See Maps of Museums and Art Sites, pages 206–209.

B Maurice Utrillo, *Street in Paris,*
1914, oil on canvas, 25 in. × 31 in. Helen Birch Bartlett Memorial Collection, The Art Institute of Chicago, Chicago, Illinois.

Trace with your finger the lines that form the sides of the road in image **B**. How did the artist make the road appear to extend into the distance? Use the diagram at the right to help you see how the artist used linear perspective.

Look at the white building on the left side of image **B**. How did the artist use linear perspective to show the depth of this building? Compare the sizes of the windows on the side of the building. How did the artist use proportion to make the building appear to extend into the distance?

With linear perspective, lines converge to show distance.

103

If you look down a road that reaches the horizon, the sides of the road appear to meet at a point. This point on the horizon is called the **vanishing point**. Find the vanishing point in image C.

Compare the sizes of the telephone poles in image C. Notice where the bottom of each pole is placed. Where else did the artist of image C use proportion and placement to show distance?

Think Critically

1. (Focus Skill) **READING SKILL** What is the main idea of the scene in image B? What details support that main idea? **MAIN IDEA AND DETAILS**

2. Name all the places where you see linear perspective in image A.

3. **WRITE** Describe the sights, sounds, and smells you think you would experience on the road in image C.

Artist's Workshop

Draw a Street Scene

MATERIALS

- white paper
- ruler
- pencil
- colored pencils

PLAN

Think about how you can use linear perspective to create a sense of distance in a street scene.

CREATE

1. Use a ruler to draw a horizon line across your paper. Mark a vanishing point on the line. To create a road, draw diagonal lines from the bottom of the page to the vanishing point.

2. To draw the side of a building, draw two lines that start at the side of the paper and converge toward the vanishing point. Make the bottom edge of the building parallel to the side of the road.

3. Finish your drawing with colored pencils.

REFLECT

Explain how you used linear perspective to create a sense of depth in your drawing.

The vertical lines in your drawing should be parallel to the left and right edges of your paper.

John J. Audubon

Who was this country's first great science illustrator?

Nearly a century before George Washington Carver, another young American had a love of science, great powers of observation, and fine artistic skills. His name was John James Audubon.

In the early nineteenth century, Audubon toured the American wilderness, creating hundreds of drawings of birds and other animals. Books of his artwork became very popular in the United States and Europe. These books remain popular today. Most people will never see Audubon's animals in the wild, but they can see them in his careful drawings.

A

John James Audubon,
Louisiana Tanager and Scarlet Tanager,
1837, aquatint engraving,
38 in. x 26 in. Private collection.

Audubon's work shows his knowledge of science and his artistic skills. In image **A**, Audubon captured the colorful details of two types of birds. In image **B**, he illustrated the swift fox in its natural habitat.

Scientific illustrations record the sizes, colors, markings, and other details of plants and animals. This information helps scientists answer many questions about plants and animals and the habitats in which they live.

Audubon's drawings showed people the wildlife they had never seen. Many of the creatures that Audubon saw now live on only in his scientific illustrations.

B John James Audubon, *Swift Fox,* 1848, lithograph, 22 in. x 28 in. Academy of Natural Sciences, Philadelphia, Pennsylvania.

Think About Art

Artists do not use creative techniques or unusual styles when they draw scientific illustrations. Why do you think this is so?

Multimedia Biographies
Visit *The Learning Site*
www.harcourtschool.com

DID YOU KNOW?

Today, science illustrators work in industries such as publishing, research, and education. Many museums nationwide, including the National Museum of Natural History in Washington, D.C., also employ science illustrators.

National Museum of Natural History in Washington, D.C.

Outdoor Art

Many sculptures are displayed outdoors, but only a few are made to blend in with their outdoor environments. This kind of **environmental art** is sometimes called *earthworks art* or *land art*.

Part of the huge sculpture in image **A** is carved from rock in the environment. How did the sculptor make the statue blend in with its surroundings?

 Giambologna,
Apennine,
1570–80, rock, lava,
stucco, 32 ft. high.
Villa Demidoff,
Pratolino, Italy.

Installations

Image shows an outdoor installation. An **installation** is an artwork that is made to be placed in a specific indoor or outdoor environment. The location becomes part of the artwork itself. In image B, the reflection of the fish is part of the artwork. What part of the environment did the artist use as an art material?

Karl Ciesluk,
Glass Fish,
1993, broken glass and water, 12 in. high. Ottawa, Canada.

Social Studies Link

The ice pyramids in image D stand in the northernmost region of the world, above the Arctic Circle.

Arctic Circle

Temporary Sculptures

Images C and D show examples of earthworks art. These artworks were created in a natural setting with only natural materials. What materials do you see in images C and D?

Many natural artworks are temporary. An assemblage like the one in image C must be carefully photographed as soon as the artist completes it. Often, photographs are all that remain of these natural artworks.

 Andy Goldsworthy, *Broken Pebbles,* 1997, pebbles and earth. Dumfriesshire, Scotland.

 Andy Goldsworthy, *Ice Pyramids,* 1980–2000. Arctic Circle.

Think Critically

1. **READING SKILL** Describe the main idea in image A. What details support this main idea? **MAIN IDEA AND DETAILS**

2. What effects do you think weather would have on the artworks in images C and D?

3. **WRITE** Describe the steps you would take to build ice sculptures like the ones in image D.

Artist's Workshop

Create a Natural Sculpture

MATERIALS

- natural objects
- scissors
- poster board
- glue

PLAN

Collect natural materials such as leaves, stones, or shells. Think about how you can use the materials to create a natural sculpture.

CREATE

1. Cut an organic shape from a piece of poster board.

2. Arrange your natural objects on the poster board. When you find the best arrangement, glue the objects down.

3. Carry your sculpture outside. Find a place where it blends in with its surroundings. You may want to take a photograph of it before you bring it back inside.

REFLECT

Tell why you chose the materials in your sculpture. Why did you arrange them the way you did?

Safety Tips

Remember to point scissors away from you as you cut.

Unit 3 Review and Reflect

Vocabulary and Concepts

Choose the letter of the word or phrase that best completes each sentence.

1 The ___ line is where the land and sky appear to meet.

  A contour   **C** horizon

  B wavy   **D** gesture

2 ___ is the empty area between and around objects.

  F Shape   **H** Movement

  G Space   **J** Color

3 The scattering of light in the atmosphere is called ___.

  A diffusion   **C** perspective

  B emphasis   **D** movement

4 When artists use ___ perspective, they make parallel lines converge in the distance.

  F atmospheric   **H** color

  G horizon   **J** linear

5 Artists use proportion and ___ to create a sense of depth in artworks.

  A movement   **C** shape

  B placement   **D** form

READING SKILL

Main Idea and Details

Reread the third paragraph on page 96. Use a diagram like this one to help you identify the main idea of the paragraph. Include details that support the main idea.

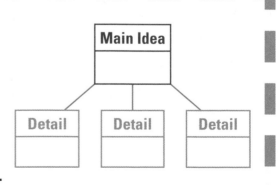

Write About Art

Write a paragraph that explains the main idea of an artwork in a previous unit. Use a diagram to organize your ideas. Write one sentence explaining the main idea. Write two or three sentences describing the details that support the main idea.

REMEMBER — YOU SHOULD

- tell what the artwork is mainly about.

- try to use unit vocabulary words.

- use correct grammar, spelling, and punctuation.

Critic's Corner

Look at the painting below to answer these questions.

DESCRIBE How would you describe the details in this artwork? What is its subject?

ANALYZE How does the artist use color to direct your eyes around this painting? What do you see first? What do you see next?

INTERPRET What mood or feeling do you think the artist wanted to express in this artwork?

EVALUATE Do you think the artist successfully used color and movement to express a mood in this artwork? Explain your answer.

André Derain, *Charing Cross Bridge,*
1906, oil on canvas, 81 cm x 100 cm. Musée d'Orsay, Paris, France.

Jenne Magafan, *Cowboy Dance* (mural study),
1941, oil on fiberboard, $23\frac{7}{8}$ in. × $30\frac{3}{4}$ in.

LOCATE IT

This painting can be found at the Smithsonian American Art Museum in Washington, D.C.

See Maps of Museums and Art Sites, pages 206–209.

Washington, D.C.

Looking at Ourselves

Step into the Art

Imagine going to the dance shown in the painting.
As you enter the room, where would you stand?
What kind of music would you hear? Would you
start to dance? If not, what would you do?

ABOUT THE ARTIST

See Gallery
of Artists,
pages 240–253.

Unit Vocabulary

narrative art	self-portrait	bust
pose	focal point	symbol
figure	tactile texture	Cubism
portrait	visual texture	profile
expression	classical art	
facial features	ideal form	

GO ONLINE

Multimedia Art Glossary
Visit *The Learning Site*
www.harcourtschool.com

Narrative Elements

Narrative elements are the parts of a narrative, or story. Every story has a setting, one or more characters, and a plot.

You can find narrative elements in many artworks. Look for them in the painting below.

- The **setting** is a ballroom during James Madison's presidency, between 1809 and 1817.

- The **characters** are First Lady Dolley Madison, President James Madison, and their guests.

- The **plot**, or action, includes the First Lady and the President receiving two British flags. The scene may represent the American victory over the British in the War of 1812.

Jennie Augusta Brownscombe, *Dolley Madison's Ball,* 1900, oil on canvas, 27 in. × 36 in. The Louise & Alan Sellars Collection of Art by American Women, Indianapolis, Indiana.

116

Being able to identify the setting, characters, and plot in a story can help you understand it better. Read the story below, and think about its narrative elements.

Lucy and her father rode in a carriage through the muddy streets of Washington. Lucy had been worrying for hours, but her father assured her, "Don't worry, Lucy. You will make a fine impression on the President."

"But what about the First Lady, Father? What will she think of me if my shoes are caked with mud?"

Lucy's father laughed. "She will pay no mind to that at all. The First Lady will be delighted to meet you."

Lucy was not convinced, but by now it was too late. The carriage stopped in front of the White House. Lucy looked out and, to her great relief, saw a dry wooden walkway leading from the carriage to the door.

Use a story map like this one to describe the setting, characters, and plot of this story.

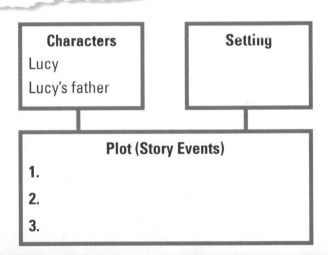

Characters
Lucy
Lucy's father

Setting

Plot (Story Events)
1.
2.
3.

On Your Own

As you look at the artworks in this unit, think about the stories the artists are telling. Use story maps to keep track of the narrative elements. Look back at your story maps when you see questions with ⭐ Focus Skill *READING SKILL* .

Narrative Art

Art that tells a story is called **narrative art**. A narrative artwork includes a setting, characters, and actions from one moment in a story. Image **A** shows the moment in 1848 when gold was discovered at Sutter's Mill in California. Describe the characters and setting you see in this painting. What actions are shown in the scene? What do you think happened before and after the moment shown in the painting?

To make a scene look realistic, artists make sketches of live models. A model stands in a frozen position, or **pose**, to represent each character in the scene. Then the sketches are combined into the finished artwork. Describe the different poses you see in image **A**.

 Constantino Brumidi and Filippo Costaggini,
Discovery of Gold in California **(detail),**
1889, fresco, 8 ft. 3 in. high. U.S. Capitol Rotunda, Washington, D.C.

The narrative artwork in image **B** is an illustration from the story "Sleeping Beauty." In the story a princess falls into a deep sleep, and a prince must kiss her in order to wake her. Look at image **B**. What do you think will happen next?

Proportion

Artists follow simple rules to draw the parts of the human body, or **figure**, in correct proportion. Look at the figure proportions diagram below. The basic unit of measurement is the height of a person's head. Arms and legs are about three "heads" long.

Average adults are between seven and eight heads high, but in some paintings, a hero or king may be nine heads high. Why do you think artists make these figures taller?

 Jessie Willcox Smith,
Sleeping Beauty and the Prince,
book illustration.

Figure Proportions

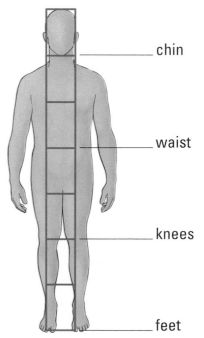

chin

waist

knees

feet

119

LOCATE IT

Many of Norman Rockwell's paintings can be found at the Norman Rockwell Museum in Stockbridge, Massachusetts.

MASSACHUSETTS

Stockbridge

See Maps of Museums and Art Sites, pages 206–209.

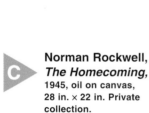

Norman Rockwell, *The Homecoming,* 1945, oil on canvas, 28 in. × 22 in. Private collection.

The World War II poster in image **C** used a narrative painting to persuade people to invest money in the war effort. The painting shows a soldier coming home from war. How would you describe the characters? Why do you think the government chose this painting to support its message?

Think Critically

1. **READING SKILL** Who do you think is the most important character in image **A**? Explain your answer. **NARRATIVE ELEMENTS**

2. Describe the setting of image **B**.

3. **WRITE** Choose two characters in image **C**, and describe what they would do next if you could "unfreeze" the action.

120

Artist's Workshop

Make an Action Figure Flip Book

MATERIALS

- white paper
- scissors
- pencil
- black marker
- stapler

PLAN

Think about a figure in action. Work with a partner who will model each pose.

CREATE

1. Fold two sheets of paper into quarters, and then cut them into eight equal pieces.

2. On one piece, make a quick sketch of a classmate in a standing position.

3. Have your classmate change position to show that he or she is beginning to walk. Your classmate should change position six more times. Sketch each pose on a different piece of paper.

4. Outline each figure with black marker. Staple your drawings together and flip through the pages. The figure will appear to walk.

REFLECT

Describe the way your figure moves. What could you do to make the action smoother?

Quick Tip

Use these figures as a guide.

Portraits

Diego Velázquez,
Juan de Pareja,
1650, oil on canvas,
81.3 cm × 70 cm.
Metropolitan Museum of
Art, New York, New York.

A **portrait** is a two-dimensional or three-dimensional artwork whose subject is a person. Portrait artists pay close attention to facial **expression**, or the look on the subject's face. They carefully pose the person's body to help show his or her personality. Describe the expression and pose of the subject in image **A**. What do they tell you about his personality?

When image **A** was painted, only noblemen wore white lace collars. However, the man in image **A** was the painter's assistant. Why do you think the artist chose to paint his assistant dressed as a nobleman?

The subject of the three-dimensional portrait in image **B** looks shockingly real. Artist Duane Hanson created the exact likeness of his subject by using a body mold. He applied liquid plastic to the subject's face and body. When the plastic dried, it was removed in sections, reassembled, and painted.

What do the expression and pose of the subject in image **B** tell you about him? What do his clothes tell you?

Look at the portrait in image **C**. Why do you think horses and buildings were included in this portrait? What do the boy's expression and pose tell you about him? What kind of personality do you think the boy has?

B Duane Hanson, *Football Player,*
1981, oil on polyvinyl, 43 in. × 28 in. × 36 in.
Lowe Art Museum, University of Miami, Miami, Florida.

LOCATE IT

The sculpture in image **B** can be found at the Lowe Art Museum in Miami, Florida.

FLORIDA

Miami

See Maps of Museums and Art Sites, pages 206–209.

C Roberto Montenegro,
Boy with Horses,
1941, oil on canvas,
29 in. × 26 in.

123

Look at the portrait in image **D**. The artist used very few brushstrokes to show a child's facial features. **Facial features** include the eyes, the nose, the mouth, and the ears. What do you think the child in image **D** is feeling? How do her facial features express her feelings?

Facial Proportions

Artists use diagrams like this one to draw the parts of the face in correct proportion. The eyes are halfway between the top of the head and the chin. The corners of the mouth are under the pupils of the eyes. How long are the ears in comparison to the nose?

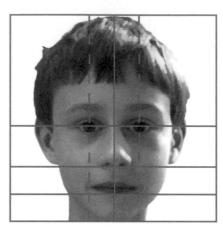

▽ **D** **Mary Cassatt,** *Head of a Young Girl.* Private collection, Paris, France.

Think Critically

1. **(Focus Skill) READING SKILL** The subject of image **A** was a painter's assistant. What do you think he normally wore in the artist's studio? **NARRATIVE ELEMENTS**

2. What other poses might the artist have chosen for the portrait in image **B**?

3. **WRITE** Ask a classmate to model a proud, angry, or sad expression. Describe how the facial features express that feeling.

Artist's Workshop

Paint a Watercolor Portrait

MATERIALS

- white paper
- pencil
- ruler
- watercolors
- water cup
- paintbrush

PLAN

Ask a classmate to be the subject of a portrait you will paint. Think about a pose that will tell something about your classmate's personality.

CREATE

1. Sketch the contour lines of your subject. Lightly draw the guidelines you see in the diagram of facial proportions on page 124.

2. Carefully draw the shape of each facial feature to make the portrait look as much like your classmate as possible.

3. Use watercolors to complete your portrait.

REFLECT

Describe the way you used proportion in your portrait. How did you show something about your subject's personality?

Quick Tip

Erase guidelines before painting.

WESTERN HEROES IN ART

How did artists tell the story of the American West in the late 1800s and early 1900s?

The brave men and women who lived on the Western frontier in the nineteenth century were often shown in traditional artworks, such as drawings, paintings, and sculptures. Then artists found new ways to capture these Western heroes in dime novels and moving pictures.

Moving pictures—also known as *movies*, *motion pictures*, and *films*—became popular in the United States at the beginning of the twentieth century. A former cowhand named Tom Mix was one of the first stars. Mix and his horse, Tony, appeared in more than 200 moving pictures such as the one advertised in image **A**.

 Moving picture poster, 1914.

B Beadle's Dime New York Library, book cover, 1884.

Movies replaced popular books known as dime novels, adventure stories that cost ten cents to buy. The novel shown in image **B** is set in Texas. Its main character is a female hero, and it was written by one of the most famous Western heroes of all time, Colonel Buffalo Bill Cody. What do you think the plot of this dime novel may have been?

THINK ABOUT ART

Describe the characters, setting, and plot in image **A**.

DID YOU KNOW?

Americans' love of the old West continued with the first television shows in the 1950s. Roy Rogers, the "King of the Cowboys," was one of television's first Western heroes. Roy Rogers, his wife Dale Evans, and his horse Trigger were seen in millions of homes every week. Roy Rogers dolls, toys, and lunchboxes are still popular collectors' items today.

Roy Rogers lunchbox

Self-Portraits

Vocabulary

self-portrait

focal point

tactile texture

visual texture

In a **self-portrait**, the artist is also the subject. One way artists create self-portraits is by sketching what they see in a mirror. They use different methods to tell viewers about their lives and personalities.

Focal Point

Look at image **A**. What is the largest object in the painting? Why do you think the artist made her own image so small? The **focal point** of a painting is the place where viewers stop and focus their attention. What is the focal point of the painting in image **A**?

Frida Kahlo, the artist of image **B**, often included Mexican plants and animals in her self-portraits to show her love for her homeland, Mexico. What is the focal point of image **B**?

 GG Kopilak, *Self-Portrait in Iron,* 1980, oil on canvas, 26 in. × 34 in. Private collection.

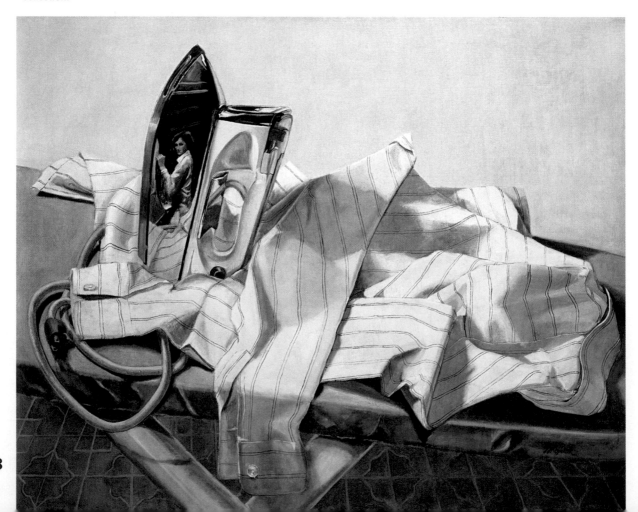

Frida Kahlo,
Fulang Chang and I,
1937, oil on composition board
with painted mirror frame,
$22\frac{1}{4}$ in. × $17\frac{3}{8}$ in. × $1\frac{3}{4}$ in.
Museum of Modern Art,
New York, New York.

Compare the sizes of the subjects in images **A** and **B**. Now compare the settings of the paintings. What can you tell about each artist from her self-portrait?

Tactile and Visual Texture

What would the objects in image **A** feel like if you could touch them? The surface of a real object has a **tactile texture**. It may be hard, soft, rough, or smooth. When artists show the look of tactile texture, they create **visual texture**.

Describe the visual texture of the iron in image **A**. How did the artist create that texture? What visual textures do you see in image **B**?

LOCATE IT

The self-portrait in image C can be found at the Van Gogh Museum in Amsterdam, the Netherlands.

Amsterdam

THE NETHERLANDS

See Maps of Museums and Art Sites, pages 206–209.

Artists may create self-portraits that show their moods and feelings. What mood do you think the artist was trying to show in image C?

Look at the short, choppy lines in the background of image C. Do you think they represent a real setting or a feeling? Look at the lines in the painter's hat and beard. What kind of visual texture do they create?

Think Critically

1. **READING SKILL** What do you think happened just before the artist painted image A? What do you think will happen next? **NARRATIVE ELEMENTS**

2. How would you change the lines and colors in image C to show a calm, peaceful mood?

3. **WRITE** Write a short story, using the setting and characters you see in image B.

Vincent van Gogh,
Self-Portrait with Straw Hat,
1887, oil on canvas, 40.5 cm × 32 cm.
Van Gogh Museum, Amsterdam,
the Netherlands.

Artist's Workshop

Make a Self-Portrait Print

MATERIALS

- mirror
- white paper
- pencil
- foam plate
- ballpoint pen
- tempera paint
- foam brush

PLAN

Think about how you can use visual texture in a self-portrait print.

CREATE

1. Look in a mirror, and draw your own face, neck, and shoulders.

2. Use a ballpoint pen to copy your drawing onto a foam plate. Press hard enough to indent the lines into the foam.

3. Use a foam brush to apply paint to the plate. Make sure the paint does not seep into the lines.

4. Place a clean sheet of paper over the foam. Press evenly to transfer the paint to the paper. Pull off the paper.

REFLECT

Describe the visual texture in your self-portrait.

Quick Tip

Use a book or another flat object to press evenly on the paper when you are making the print.

Sculptural Portraits

Since ancient times artists have created three-dimensional portraits out of stone, clay, and other materials. Image **A** shows part of Michelangelo's statue *David*. A statue is a sculpture that shows all of a figure.

The sculpture in image **A** is one of the finest examples of classical art. **Classical art** is made in the style of ancient Greek and Roman art. Such works show the **ideal form**, or the perfect form, of their subjects. The ideal is not necessarily realistic. Look at the curls in the subject's hair in image **A**. Do they look realistic, or do they look too perfect to be real?

Michelangelo,
***David* (detail),**
1501–1504, marble,
14 ft. high. Galleria
dell'Accademia,
Florence, Italy.

The artist of image **B** did not create an ideal form in this self-portrait. Rather, he showed a realistic view of himself. Compare the curls in the hair in image **B** with those in image **A**. Compare the facial features in image **B** with those in image **A**.

The self-portrait in image **B** is in the form of a **bust**. A bust is a sculpture showing a person's head and neck and sometimes the upper body.

B ▷ **Giovanni Lorenzo Bernini,**
Portrait of Bernini,
1680s, bronze, 46 cm. high.
Hermitage Museum,
St. Petersburg, Russia.

Social Studies Link

In A.D. 900, the Mayan civilization stretched across thousands of miles in present-day Central America.

NORTH AMERICA

Mayan civilization, Central America

The man's face shown in image C was carved more than 1,000 years ago by a Mayan artist. The king's head shown in image D was made in Africa more than 500 years ago.

Describe the texture of the face in image C. Do you think the texture was made by the artist or by nature? The artist of image D carved one texture into the face and other textures into the crown. How would you describe these textures?

D Unknown artist, Portrait head of a king, about A.D. 1100–1300, terra-cotta with traces of red pigment, 9 in. high. Kimball Art Museum, Fort Worth, Texas.

 Unknown artist, Male face, about A.D. 700–900, stucco with traces of paint, 26 cm × 22.7 cm × 16.5 cm. Kimball Art Museum, Fort Worth, Texas.

Think Critically

1. **Focus Skill** *READING SKILL* How can you tell that the character in image D is a king? **NARRATIVE ELEMENTS**

2. Would you prefer to be sculpted in the style of image A or in the style of image B? Explain why.

3. **WRITE** Describe how the self-portrait in image B could be changed to an ideal form.

Artist's Workshop

Sculpt a Clay Portrait

MATERIALS

- ball of clay
- sculpting tools
- additional clay

PLAN

Think about a face you would like to sculpt. You may choose someone you know or someone from your imagination.

CREATE

1. Push and pull a round ball of clay into the shape of a head. Smooth the back of the shape so that it lies flat.

2. Use a pencil to lightly draw guidelines on the clay. Refer to the facial proportions diagram on page 124.

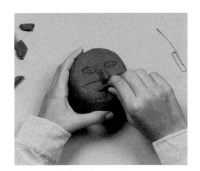

3. Use additional pieces of clay to build up the cheeks, nose, lips, and eyebrows. Add extra clay to make the hair. Use a tool to carve texture into the hair.

REFLECT

Tell how you created texture in the clay.

Quick Tip

To dry thoroughly, clay should be no more than four inches thick. If necessary, hollow out the back of the form before drying.

Vinnie Ream

Who was the first woman to have her artwork displayed in the United States Capitol?

A George Peter Alexander Healy, *Portrait of Vinnie Ream,* about 1870, oil on canvas, $31\frac{3}{8}$ in. x $22\frac{1}{2}$ in.

B Vinnie Ream with her marble sculpture, *Bust of Lincoln,* in 1865

In 1861, when she was fourteen, Vinnie Ream moved with her family from the Wisconsin wilderness to the capital city of Washington, D.C. Shortly after that, she took up the art of sculpture. Her talent was quickly recognized and soon she was creating busts of members of Congress. This led to an even greater experience— Vinnie Ream was asked to create a bust of President Abraham Lincoln for the White House. Lincoln himself agreed to pose for her.

After Abraham Lincoln was assassinated in 1865, Vinnie Ream was chosen by Congress to create a statue of him for the Capitol. She was only eighteen years old. She became the youngest person, and the first woman of any age, to have her work displayed in the Capitol's National Statuary Hall.

Vinnie Ream sculpted many other famous Americans, including Admiral David Farragut and Cherokee leader Sequoya, and she was herself the subject of many painters and photographers.

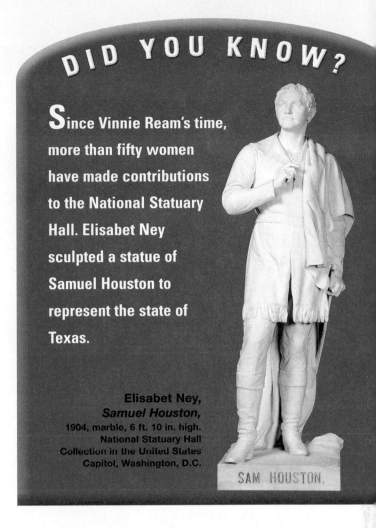

Since Vinnie Ream's time, more than fifty women have made contributions to the National Statuary Hall. Elisabet Ney sculpted a statue of Samuel Houston to represent the state of Texas.

Elisabet Ney,
Samuel Houston,
1904, marble, 6 ft. 10 in. high.
National Statuary Hall
Collection in the United States
Capitol, Washington, D.C.

Vinnie Ream,
Abraham Lincoln,
1871, marble, 83 in. high.
U.S. Capitol Rotunda,
Washington, D.C.

Think About Art

If you could honor a famous person from history by sculpting his or her portrait, who would it be? Why would you choose that person?

Multimedia Biographies
Visit *The Learning Site*
www.harcourtschool.com

137

Unusual Portraits

Giuseppe Arcimboldo, *Spring,* 1573, oil on canvas, 30 in. × 25 in. Musée du Louvre, Paris, France.

Artists have always used their imaginations to create unusual portraits. Image **A** was painted more than 400 years ago. Look closely at its subject. What do you see? Look at the nose and the ear. What objects are they?

This painting is filled with symbols. A **symbol** is something used by an artist to stand for something else. In image **A** the flowers, fruits, and vegetables represent spring, the season of blooming and growth.

Abstract Portraits

The abstract portrait in image **B** was created 340 years after image **A**. This artist also used symbols. The gears and smokestacks represent a world full of machines and factories. Can you point out a man's eyes, nose, and mouth?

This painting is part of an art movement called Cubism. In **Cubism** parts of the subject are simplified into geometric shapes and then rearranged. What do you think the artist wanted to show about his subject's life and personality?

Social Studies Link

The artist of image **B** was interested in the industrial revolution that began in his home country of Russia in the late 1800s. The industrial revolution in the United States began 100 years earlier, in the late 1700s.

B Kasimir Malevich, *Portrait of the Artist, I. Klyun,* 1913, oil on canvas, 112 cm × 70 cm. Russisches Museum, St. Petersburg, Russia.

Now look at the Cubist portrait in image **C**. The artist has shown two views of her subject at the same time. Point out the facial features in the front view. The right side of this painting shows a **profile**, or side view of the subject. Where are the facial features in the side view?

Think Critically

1. (Focus Skill) **READING SKILL** What kind of personality do you think the subject of image **C** has? **NARRATIVE ELEMENTS**

2. How would you describe the textures in images **A** and **B**?

3. **WRITE** Choose a season or a time of year that you could represent in a portrait. Describe what objects you would use as symbols for that season.

C Brianna, age 10, Untitled.

Artist's Workshop

Draw an Abstract Portrait

MATERIALS

- **white paper**
- **pencil**
- **colored markers**

PLAN

Sketch the front view of a classmate's face. Then make a separate sketch of your classmate's profile.

CREATE

1. **Combine the two sketches into one pencil drawing. Show both a front view and a side view of your subject at the same time.**

2. **Draw straight or wavy lines across the paper, dividing your portrait into sections. Add more lines and shapes to create patterns in each section.**

3. **Finish your drawing with colored markers.**

REFLECT

Describe how the proportions of your abstract portrait are different from those of a realistic portrait.

Quick Tip

You may want to use symbols in your abstract portrait to tell something about your subject.

141

Unit 4 Review and Reflect

Vocabulary and Concepts

Choose the letter of the word or phrase that best completes each sentence.

1 ___ artworks include settings, characters, and actions.

A Narrative   C Clay

B Abstract   D Stone

2 The eyes, nose, and mouth are examples of ___.

F textures   H subjects

G facial features   J patterns

3 Viewers stop and focus their attention on an artwork's ___.

A setting   C focal point

B shape   D form

4 Images that artists create of themselves are called ___.

F self-portraits   H portraits

G symbols   J designs

5 You can feel a real object's ___.

A visual texture   C color

B tactile texture   D value

 **READING SKILL**

Narrative Elements

Read the story written by a classmate about the image on page 129. Use a story map to identify the characters, setting, and plot in your classmate's story.

Characters	Setting

Plot (Story Events)
1.
2.
3.

Write About Art

Choose an artwork from this unit to use as the basis for a story. Pick an artwork with a setting and two characters. Include the action shown in the artwork in the plot of your story.

REMEMBER — YOU SHOULD

- include details about the characters and setting.

- include a series of actions or events.

- use correct grammar, spelling, and punctuation.

Critic's Corner

Look at *The Quarry Worker* by Diego Rivera to answer the questions below.

DESCRIBE What type of artwork is it? What is its subject?

ANALYZE Describe the visual textures in the artwork.

INTERPRET Describe the subject's facial expression and pose. What do they tell you about his feelings and about his work?

EVALUATE What is your opinion of the way the artist portrayed his subject?

Diego Rivera,
The Quarry Worker,
1944, watercolor on
paper, $15\frac{3}{8}$ in. × $10\frac{7}{8}$ in.
Private collection.

Winslow Homer, *Kissing the Moon*,
1904, oil on canvas, 30 in. × 40 in.

LOCATE IT

This painting can be found at the Addison Gallery of
American Art, Phillips Academy, in Andover,
Massachusetts.

See Maps of Museums and Art Sites, pages 206–209.

A Balancing Act

Step into the Art

Look at the title of this artwork. What do you think it means? How would you describe the ocean waves? If you could join the men in the boat, what might you feel, see, hear, and taste? What kinds of emotions might you feel?

Unit Vocabulary

visual weight	quadrant pattern	diagonals
vertical axis	horizontal axis	sequential
symmetrical balance	radial balance	Golden Rectangle
exact symmetry	asymmetrical balance	intensity
near symmetry	contrast	neutral colors
unity	shading	dominant color
		continuous lines

ABOUT THE ARTIST

See Gallery of Artists, pages 240–253.

 Multimedia Art Glossary
Visit *The Learning Site*
www.harcourtschool.com

Fact and Opinion

A *fact* is a statement that can be proved. An *opinion* is someone's belief about something. An opinion cannot be proved.

Look at the painting *My San Francisco*.

- It is a fact that the city of San Francisco has many hills.

- It is a fact that the city has bridges, churches, and places to sail a boat.

- It is an opinion that San Francisco is an active, happy place. Viewers can tell that the artist has this opinion, because she uses vibrant colors and shows energetic activities.

Patricia A. Schwimmer,
My San Francisco,
1994, tempera on paper,
20 in. × 26 in. Private collection.

Knowing how to tell a fact from an opinion can help you understand what you read. Read this passage, and think about what could be proved and what could not be proved.

Visit San Francisco

San Francisco is the best city in the United States. It is located on the coast of California, about halfway up the state. San Francisco is a city of 46 square miles, and every square mile is worth visiting. The 750,000 residents of this city will welcome you with a smile.

Fill in this chart by listing the **facts** on the left side and the **opinions** on the right side.

Facts	Opinions
on the coast of California	best city in the United States

On Your Own

As you read the lessons in this unit, use charts like the one above to separate facts from opinions. Look back at your charts when you see questions with (Focus Skill) *READING SKILL* .

Vocabulary

visual weight

vertical axis

symmetrical balance

exact symmetry

near symmetry

Symmetrical Compositions

When we stand, walk, or ride a bicycle, we balance our weight evenly on the left and right sides of our bodies. Artists balance the **visual weight**, or emphasis, of elements on the left and right sides of an artwork.

Symmetrical Balance

Imagine a vertical line drawn through the center of image **A**. This line is the **vertical axis**. Do the objects on each side of the vertical axis have equal emphasis? Are the shapes and colors on the left similar to those on the right? Those similarities give the painting **symmetrical balance**.

 Unknown artist, *Menorah* (detail), before 1982, stained glass window. Rabbinate Synagogue, Jerusalem, Israel.

Exact Symmetry and Near Symmetry

When one half of an artwork exactly matches the other half, it has perfect balance, or **exact symmetry**. Look again at image **A**. Do the shapes on the two sides of the vertical axis match exactly? Do the colors match? Does this artwork have exact symmetry?

LOCATE IT

The sculpture in image **B** is carved into a temple wall in Selinus, an ancient city on the southern coast of the island of Sicily.

ITALY

Sicily

See Maps of Museums and Art Sites, pages 206–209.

B Unknown artist, *The Chariot of Apollo,* about 550 B.C., limestone. Temple C at Selinus Archaeological Museum, Palermo, Italy.

Now look at the sculpture in image **B**. How many horses are on each side of the vertical axis? Are the horses exactly the same? Look at the chariot driver. Compare the visual weight of the objects in his left and right hands. Image **B** is an example of **near symmetry**. The elements in this artwork are carefully balanced, but they are not exactly the same on the left and the right.

Look at the arrangement of shapes in image . Picture the vertical axis of this composition. Do the objects on the left and right sides have equal emphasis? Do the colors and shapes on the left and right sides match exactly? Does the artwork in image C have exact symmetry or near symmetry?

Henri Matisse, *Christmas Eve,* 1952, gouache on cut and pasted paper, 10 ft. 7 in. × 53 in. Museum of Modern Art, New York, New York.

Think Critically

1. (Focus Skill) *READING SKILL* "The artwork in image C seems festive." Is this statement a fact or an opinion? **FACT AND OPINION**

2. State two things the artist could have done to make the sculpture in image B show exact symmetry.

3. **WRITE** Find an object in your classroom that has exact symmetry. Write a paragraph to describe three ways in which the left and right sides of the object match.

150

Artist's Workshop

Create a Symmetrical Composition

MATERIALS

- white paper
- pencil
- black crayon
- oil pastels

PLAN

Think about how you can use lines and shapes in a symmetrical composition. Decide whether you will create exact symmetry or near symmetry.

CREATE

1. Fold your paper in half vertically, and open it up. Sketch a variety of shapes on one side of the vertical axis. Outline your shapes with black crayon.

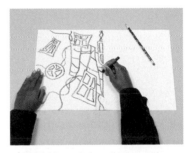

2. Refold your paper, and rub it to transfer the crayon marks to the other side of the page. Open your paper and darken the transferred outlines where needed.

3. Color your design with oil pastels.

REFLECT

Explain how you created exact symmetry or near symmetry.

Quick Tip

You may want to center some shapes on the vertical axis.

Symmetrical Patterns

Images **A** and **B** are separated in time by more than 1,000 years. However, both artworks show two of the timeless principles of art—symmetry and unity. **Unity** is a quality of wholeness or completeness in an artwork. Look at the shapes in image **A**. How do they fit together in a way that shows unity? Which of the shapes could you take away and still have an artwork that is whole and complete?

 Unknown artist,
Back cover of
The Lindau Gospels,
late eighth century, gilt
silver, enamel and jewels.
The Pierpont Morgan Library,
New York, New York.

152

Quadrant Patterns

Images **A** and **B** show quadrant patterns. A **quadrant pattern** is divided into four sections. A vertical axis divides the quadrant into left and right halves. A **horizontal axis** divides it into top and bottom halves. Quadrant patterns are symmetrical in two directions—left to right and top to bottom.

How do the shapes in image **B** work together to create a sense of unity in this artwork? Which of the shapes could you take away and still have an artwork that is whole and complete?

 Andy Warhol, *Four Blue Hearts,* about 1979–1984, synthetic polymer paint and silkscreen ink on canvas, 15 in. × 15 in. The Andy Warhol Museum, Pittsburgh, Pennsylvania.

LOCATE IT

The stained-glass window in image C can be found in the Cathedral of Notre Dame, in Paris, France.

See Maps of Museums and Art Sites, pages 206–209.

Radial Patterns

Images C and D are separated in time by many centuries, but both artists used the same principle of radial balance to create a circular pattern. A design has **radial balance** when all its parts are balanced around a center point. Find the center point in the stained-glass window in image C. Notice the way each part of the design radiates from the center like the spokes of a wheel. Describe how the design in image D shows radial balance.

Think Critically

1. **READING SKILL** Choose an artwork from this lesson, and write one fact and one opinion about it. FACT AND OPINION

2. Look at image D. Does this artwork have exact symmetry or near symmetry? Explain your answer.

3. **WRITE** Look back at images A and B. Write a paragraph describing the differences you see between the ancient and the modern artworks.

 Unknown artist, *Rose Window,* **Notre Dame Cathedral,** thirteenth century, stained glass, 42 ft. × 30 ft. Paris, France.

 Peter, age 10, *Compass Art.*

154

Artist's Workshop

Create a Radial Design

MATERIALS

- **white paper**
- **compass**
- **pencil**
- **ruler**
- **oil pastels**

PLAN

Think about ways you can arrange lines and shapes in a radial design. Decide how you will create unity in your design.

CREATE

1. Use a compass to draw a large circle, and then divide the circle into four equal sections.

2. Draw smaller circles inside the large one, or add circles around its edge. Draw the same shapes in each of the four sections.

3. Use oil pastels to color your design. Choose colors that will help make the parts of your design fit together as a whole.

REFLECT

Tell how you used shape and color to create unity in your design.

Safety Tips

Completely close a compass when it is not in use.

SOFONISBA ANGUISSOLA

At a time when only men were recognized as artists, was it possible for a woman to join their distinguished ranks?

 Sofonisba Anguissola, *Self-Portrait,* 1554, oil on panel, 19.5 cm x 12.5 cm.

Sofonisba Anguissola (soh•foh•NIS•bah ahn•GWEES•soh•lah) was born in 1532 into a noble Italian family. She was the oldest of seven children, including six girls. It was a time when girls had few choices in life, but Sofonisba's father urged his daughters to pursue their ambitions. Sofonisba's desire was to become a great portrait painter.

Sofonisba's talent was apparent from an early age. As a teenager she studied with local artists, and then the great painter and sculptor Michelangelo saw her work and took a personal interest in her career. Michelangelo's support set Sofonisba on the path to international success. Within a few years she was living in Madrid, Spain, as a court painter for Prince Philip II.

Sofonisba Anguissola lived into her nineties, painting beautiful portraits all the while. At her death in 1625, she was one of the most admired women in Europe. Nearly 400 years later, she remains one of the best-known women artists of all time.

THINK ABOUT ART

In her portraits Sofonisba Anguissola tried to show the emotions of her subjects. What can you tell about the feelings of the children toward the father in image **B**?

 Sofonisba Anguissola, *Portrait of the Artist's Family*, about 1559, oil on canvas, 62 in. x 48 in. Nivaagaard Collection Museum, Niva, Denmark.

Multimedia Biographies
Visit *The Learning Site*
www.harcourtschool.com

Lesson
23

Vocabulary

asymmetrical
  balance

contrast

shading

Asymmetrical Balance

Many artworks are not symmetrical, because they have more shapes or larger shapes on one side than on the other side. An artwork that is not symmetrical can still be balanced. Artists use visual weight to create **asymmetrical balance** in their artworks.

Contrast and Balance

Look at image **A**. The boy's face is mostly on the left side of the vertical axis. How did the artist add visual weight to the right side to help balance the painting? Look at the strong **contrast**, or difference, between the white lines on the boy's shoulders and the dark brown background. Color contrast has great visual weight. Why do you think the artist made the shoulder stripe on the right side of the painting larger than the stripe on the left?

 Sandro Botticelli, *Portrait of a Youth,* about 1489, tempera on panel, 41 cm × 31 cm. National Gallery, Washington, D.C.

Warm Colors and Balance

Picture the vertical axis in image **B**. The largest vase is on the left side of that axis. How did the artist use color to add visual weight to the right side of the painting? Warm colors such as red and orange have more visual weight than cool colors. Does the composition seem balanced?

Light and Shadow

Point out the tints and shades on each object in image **B**. The artist used tints to show where light hit each object, and he used shades to show shadows. Artists use this kind of **shading** to make objects in two-dimensional artworks look three-dimensional.

The diagram on the right shows a light source shining on objects from the upper left corner. Notice where light hits the objects and where there is shadow. Where do you think the light source was for image **B**?

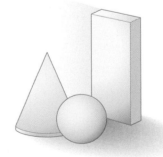

LOCATE IT

The artwork in image
C can be found at the
Musée d'Orsay in
Paris, France.

**See Maps of Museums
and Art Sites,
pages 206–209.**

Look at the still life in image **C**. Count the large and small objects on the right side of the painting. How many objects are on the left side? Does the painting have symmetrical balance? Does it have asymmetrical balance?

Notice the bright yellow fruit on the far left. How does its color help balance the painting? Look at the contrast between the white napkin and the dark background. Why do you think the artist put more of the napkin on the left side of the painting?

C Paul Cézanne,
***Still Life with
Tea Kettle,***
1869, oil on canvas,
64 cm × 81 cm. Musée
d'Orsay, Paris, France.

Think Critically

1. **Focus Skill** **READING SKILL** "The boy in image **A** is very handsome." Is this statement a fact or an opinion?
FACT AND OPINION

2. How could you rearrange the objects in image **B** and still have a balanced painting?

3. **WRITE** Choose different colors for the objects in image **C**. Describe how your color choices would keep the painting in balance.

Artist's Workshop

Paint an Asymmetrical Still Life

MATERIALS

- large and small objects
- white paper
- pencil
- watercolors
- paintbrush
- water cup

PLAN

Gather large and small objects for a still-life painting. Group several large objects together. Place smaller objects to the left of the first group.

CREATE

1. Sketch the objects that you arranged.

2. Plan a color scheme that will help balance your composition. Use bright colors to add visual weight to the small objects.

3. Finish your still life with watercolors.

REFLECT

Explain how you used color to balance your asymmetrical painting.

 Quick Tip Dull colors have less visual weight than bright colors.

Asymmetrical Compositions

Artists use several methods to compose, or arrange, the elements in an asymmetrical artwork.

Composing with Diagonals

Artists often arrange the important elements in their artworks along invisible **diagonals**, or slanted lines. Look at the asymmetrical painting in image A. Trace with your finger some invisible diagonal lines between the most brightly colored objects. Look at the diagram. How did the artist use diagonals to balance the right and left sides of the painting? How did he use color to balance the painting?

A

Edgar Degas,
Dancer on Stage,
1878, pastel and gouache
on paper, 72 cm × 77.5 cm.
Musée d'Orsay, Paris,
France.

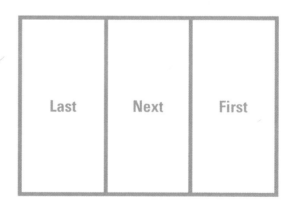

Unknown artist, *Woman Playing an Instrument,*
about 1890, Japanese wood block print, 20 in. × 16 in.
David David Gallery, Philadelphia, Pennsylvania.

Sequential Composition

Some artists arrange the elements of their
compositions in a sequence, or in steps.
Compare the **sequential** composition in
image **B** with the diagram at the right.
Where is the brightest object in image **B**?
After that object, which object do you
notice next? What do you look at last?
How did the artist use contrast and color
to balance this asymmetrical painting?

Last	Next	First

The Golden Rectangle

Since ancient times, artists have used the **Golden Rectangle** to help them compose their paintings. Look at the Golden Rectangle below. It is almost twice as wide as it is high. The smallest squares within the rectangle mark the area of greatest emphasis. Now look at image **C**. Why do you think the artist placed the boat where he did?

Edward Hopper, *The Long Leg*, 1935, oil on canvas, 20 in. × 30¼ in. The Huntington Library and Art Gallery, San Marino, California.

The Golden Rectangle

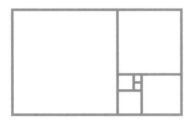

Think Critically

1. (Focus Skill) **READING SKILL** "Image **B** is an asymmetrical composition." Is this statement a fact or an opinion? **FACT AND OPINION**

2. Where did the artist of image **B** use diagonals?

3. **WRITE** Find the diagonal lines in image **C**. Then describe the kind of feeling they give the artwork.

Artist's Workshop

Paint a Sequential Composition

MATERIALS

- white paper
- pencil
- watercolors
- paintbrush
- water cup

PLAN

Imagine an outdoor scene that includes a shoreline, water, and a horizon line. Think of figures and objects you can arrange in the scene.

CREATE

1. As you sketch your scene, think of how you can guide the viewer's eyes across the painting in a certain order. Decide which objects you want the viewer to notice first, next, and last.

2. Plan the colors you will use to guide the viewer's eyes from the bottom up, from the top down, or from one side to the other.

3. Use watercolors to complete your painting.

REFLECT

Describe the sequence of your composition.

Quick Tip

Very dark colors and very bright colors catch viewers' attention first.

Copying the Colors of Nature

How do artists use minerals to create colors?

Since the time when artists made cave paintings, they have been trying to copy the colors of nature. Early artists discovered pigments, colored powders made by grinding minerals. Here are some examples of minerals that are used to make pigments:

- iron oxide for red pigment
- azurite for blue pigment
- calcite for white pigment

Some artists still use dry pigments like the ones shown in image A to mix their own paints. Pigments are mixed with oil to make oil paints or with water to make watercolors. Pigments can also be mixed with a special gum and water to form pastels, or with wax to form crayons.

Pigments on sale in a pigment shop in Nepal

Graphic artist at work at computer console

Computer artists like the one in image **B** have found new ways to copy the colors of nature. The screen of a computer monitor is lined with dots of chemicals called *phosphors*. Red, green, and blue phosphors glow when they are triggered by electronic signals. Millions of different colors are created when the computer's program electronically "mixes" these three colors.

DID YOU KNOW?

Calcite, or chalk, is a mineral that has been used by artists for more than 10,000 years to make white pigments. When seashells made of calcite build up on the ocean floor, calcite deposits are formed. Over millions of years, ocean levels may change and reveal deposits like the one below.

The white cliffs of Dover on the southeast coast of England

Think About Art

Why might the cave drawings of different regions show different colors?

167

Balance in Abstract Art

Balance and Intensity

One way that artists create balance in abstract compositions is by choosing the intensity of colors. **Intensity** is the brightness or dullness of a color. Bright colors such as yellow have high intensity. **Neutral colors** such as gray and brown have low intensity.

Look at image **A**. Where do you see mostly low-intensity colors? Where are the high-intensity colors in the painting? How did the artist use both kinds of colors to create balance in the painting in image **A**?

A Robert Delaunay, *The Runners,* about 1925, oil on canvas. Weinberg Collection, Zurich, Germany.

Dominant Color

The color with the most emphasis and visual weight in an artwork is the **dominant color**. It is the color you notice first. What is the dominant color in image **B**? Describe the intensity of this color. Point out the areas in image **B** where you see the dominant color. How did the artist distribute the dominant color in this painting to create balance?

B Louise Freshman-Brown, Untitled, 1987, pastel on paper, 30 in. × 44 In.

Intensity and Value

Look at the color strips below. They show the difference between color intensity and color value. The intensity, or brightness, of a color is reduced by adding its complement. In the first strip, the color blue was gradually added to make duller versions of orange. In the second strip, white was added to create tints of orange, and black was added to create shades of orange.

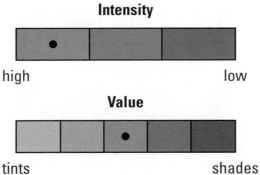

Intensity

high   low

Value

tints   shades

169

What is the dominant color in image **C**? Trace with your finger the unbroken yellow lines in this artwork. How do these **continuous lines** balance the left and right sides of the artwork?

Think Critically

1. **READING SKILL** "Image **A** shows an exciting scene." Is this statement a fact or an opinion? **FACT AND OPINION**

2. Choose one of the colors in image **B**. Point out where the artist used high intensities and low intensities of that color.

3. **WRITE** Describe what you see in image **B**, and give the painting a title.

 Mark, grade 5, Contour line painting.

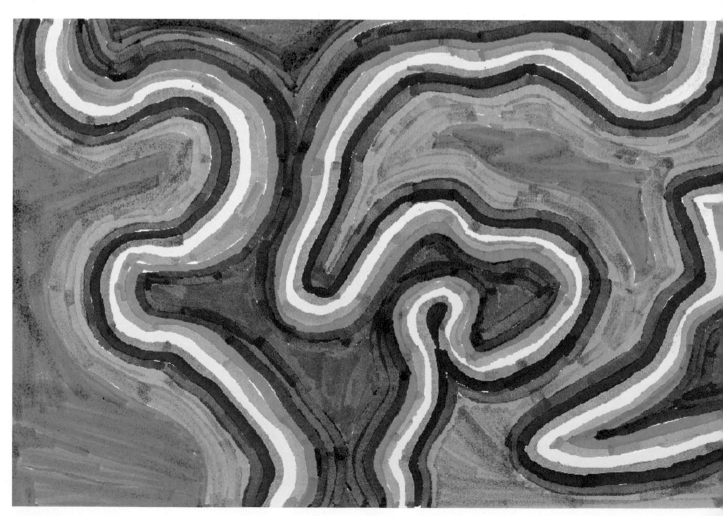

Artist's Workshop

Create an Abstract Design

MATERIALS

- **white paper**
- **colored markers**
- **pencil**

PLAN

Imagine a design you can create using continuous lines. Choose a color that you would like to use as the dominant color in your design.

CREATE

1. Use a marker to draw a continuous line that goes into each area of your paper. Draw another line around the first one, and fill in the space between them with your dominant color.

2. Choose three more colors. Use them to draw more continuous lines inside and outside your first line.

3. Continue drawing lines until you have filled your paper and no white space shows through.

REFLECT

Explain how you created balance and unity in your composition by using your dominant color.

Quick Tip

You may want to sketch the path of your continuous lines before drawing them with markers.

171

Unit 5 Review and Reflect

Vocabulary and Concepts

Choose the letter of the word or phrase that best completes each sentence.

1 In an artwork with ___, the left and right sides match exactly.

   A near symmetry   **C** visual weight

   B exact symmetry   **D** vertical axis

2 The quality of wholeness in an artwork is called ___.

   F visual weight   **H** symmetry

   G pattern   **J** unity

3 Arranging elements in a circle is a way to create ___.

   A radial balance   **C** contrast

   B diagonals   **D** shading

4 Viewers look at the parts of a ___ composition in a series of steps.

   F sequential   **H** neutral

   G radial   **J** diagonal

5 The ___ color in an artwork is the color with the most emphasis.

   A neutral   **C** dominant

   B cool   **D** pale

READING SKILL

Fact and Opinion

Reread the first paragraph on page 157 about Sofonisba Anguissola. Identify two facts and two opinions in this paragraph, and write them in a chart.

Facts	Opinions

Write About Art

Choose one artwork you have learned about in this unit, and write a paragraph describing it. Include at least two facts and two opinions in your paragraph. Use a chart to help you plan.

REMEMBER — YOU SHOULD

- state the main idea and describe the details in the artwork.

- use correct grammar, spelling, and punctuation.

Critic's Corner

Look at *Around the Cake* by Wayne Thiebaud (TEE•boh) to answer the questions below.

Wayne Thiebaud,
Around the Cake,
1962, oil on canvas,
55.9 cm × 71.1 cm. Spencer
Museum of Art, University of
Kansas, Lawrence, Kansas.

DESCRIBE What is the subject of the artwork?

ANALYZE What type of balance has the artist created? How has the artist used tints and shades?

INTERPRET How do you think the artist feels about this subject?

EVALUATE What is your opinion of the way the artist chose to show his subject?

Dale Chihuly, *Glass Boat Assemblage,*
1998, handblown glass and wooden boat, about 9 ft × 5 ft. × $5\frac{1}{2}$ ft.

LOCATE IT

This sculpture was installed at Rancho Mirage, California.

See Maps of Museums and Art Sites, pages 206–209.

CALIFORNIA
Rancho Mirage

Surprising Art

Step into the Art

Imagine that you could pick up and touch the colorful glass forms in Dale Chihuly's boat. Would they be light or heavy? Would they feel smooth or rough? Which form looks most interesting to you? Why?

Unit Vocabulary

rhythm	fiber art	Op Art
variety	benday patterns	computer-generated art
soft sculpture	art prints	digital image
pigment	engraving	highlights
neon art	optical illusions	

ABOUT THE ARTIST

See Gallery of Artists, pages 240–253.

GO ONLINE

Multimedia Art Glossary
Visit *The Learning Site*
www.harcourtschool.com

Summarize and Paraphrase

When you *summarize* a story or a work of art, you tell only the important events or ideas. When you *paraphrase* a story or a text, you retell it using different words.

Look at the artwork below. You might **summarize** the artwork like this:

• *The Tower* is a combination of familiar objects. It includes a stack of small tables, an umbrella, and a broom.

To **paraphrase** the statement above, you might say this:

• *The Tower* is made up of everyday objects. Small tables, a broom, and an umbrella are combined in an interesting way.

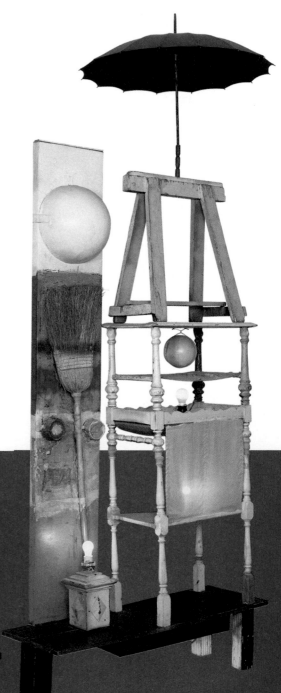

Robert Rauschenberg, *The Tower,*
1957, oil, paper, fabric, objects, and electric lights on wood
structure, 9 ft. 11 in. × 4 ft. × 2 ft. 11 in. Private collection.

Being able to summarize and paraphrase text can help you understand what you read. Read the passage below, and think about its most important ideas.

The Tower is one of Robert Rauschenberg's "combines." Rauschenberg invented this term to describe artworks made up of objects that are not usually combined. Rauschenberg often began his artworks by walking around. He picked up some of the parts for his combines, including parts for *The Tower,* on the streets of New York City.

Summarize the important ideas in the passage. Then use your own words to paraphrase the text. Use this chart to organize your ideas.

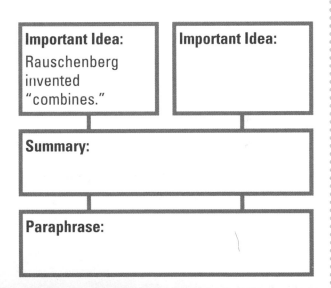

Important Idea:
Rauschenberg invented "combines."

Important Idea:

Summary:

Paraphrase:

On Your Own

As you read the lessons in this unit, use a chart like the one above to help you summarize and paraphrase what you read. Look back at your chart when you see questions with

 *READING SKILL* .

Rhythm in Sculpture

Vocabulary

rhythm

variety

soft sculpture

Rhythm is the feeling created by the regular repetition of elements in an artwork. Like a repeated drumbeat in music, repeated lines, shapes, or colors create a visual beat as the viewer's eyes move around an artwork. Artists add **variety** to artworks by using different lines, shapes, or colors.

Constructions

The artwork in image **A** is a construction, a sculpture that is constructed, or built, by joining parts together. Constructions are often made from one kind of material, such as wood. Describe the forms that make up the sculpture in image **A**. How did the artist use forms to create rhythm? Where do you see variety?

A

Louise Nevelson,
Night Landscape,
1955, wood painted black,
35½ in. × 38½ in. × 15 in.
The Museum of
Contemporary Art,
Los Angeles, California.

B Claes Oldenburg, *Floor Burger,*
1962, acrylic on canvas filled with foam rubber,
132.1 cm × 213.4 cm. Art Gallery of Ontario,
Toronto, Ontario, Canada.

Soft Sculpture

The artwork in image B is a **soft sculpture**, a sculpture made
with soft materials such as canvas and foam rubber. Claes
(KLAHS) Oldenburg was one of the first sculptors to use soft
materials in his artworks. Why do you think the artist chose
soft materials to create this artwork?

In representational artworks like the one in image B,
artists copy the shapes and colors of real objects. How do
the shapes of the pickle, bun, and meat patty create rhythm in
this artwork? How do the size and color of these objects add
variety to the sculpture?

LOCATE IT

The artwork in image
B can be found at the
Art Gallery of Ontario
in Toronto, Ontario,
Canada.

See Maps of Museums
and Art Sites,
pages 206–209.

179

Now look at image **C**. In this abstract artwork, where did the artist repeat shapes and colors to create rhythm? Where did the artist use different shapes and colors to add variety to the artwork?

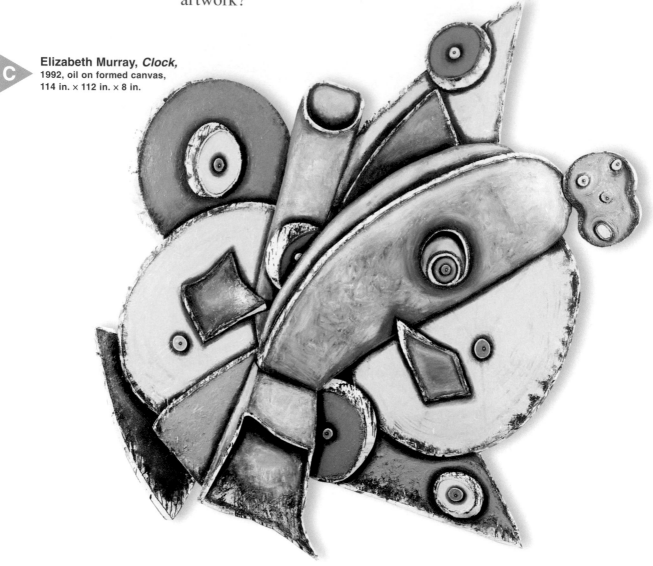

C ▶ **Elizabeth Murray,** *Clock,*
1992, oil on formed canvas,
114 in. × 112 in. × 8 in.

Think Critically

1. **(Focus Skill)** *READING SKILL* Select an artwork from this lesson. In one sentence, summarize the artwork's shapes and colors. **SUMMARIZE AND PARAPHRASE**

2. How would you feel about the sculpture in image **B** if it were all one color, like the sculpture in image **A**?

3. **WRITE** Which sculpture in this lesson do you think is the most surprising? Explain why.

180

Artist's Workshop

Create an Abstract Construction

MATERIALS

- foam plates
- scissors
- acrylic paints
- brushes
- glue

PLAN

Think of ways you can create rhythm and variety in an abstract construction. Choose a shape that you can repeat to create rhythm, and then choose a different shape that will add variety.

CREATE

1. Cut foam plates into the shapes you chose. Use tints and shades of the same color to paint the repeated shapes. Paint a foam plate and use it as a base.

2. Use a contrasting color to paint the shapes that will add variety.

3. Glue your shapes to the foam plate. Build up the construction in layers.

REFLECT

Describe how you created rhythm and variety in your construction.

Quick Tip

Glue small pieces of foam to the backs of your shapes to add space between the layers.

181

Unexpected Materials

We expect artists to use certain materials, such as paint, stone, and wood, in their artworks. Some artists, however, use those materials in unexpected ways. Others work with materials that are designed for entirely different purposes.

The surface of the artwork in image **A** is covered with **pigment**, a colored powder commonly mixed with liquid to make paint. How did the artist use this material in an unusual way? How did the artist create rhythm in this sculpture? Where did he add variety?

 Anish Kapoor, *As If to Celebrate, I Discovered a Mountain Blooming with Red Flowers,* 1981, drawing and sculpture with wood and various materials, 97 cm × 76.2 cm × 160 cm. Tate Gallery, London, England.

Neon Art

Neon lights are commonly used to make advertising signs for hotels, restaurants, and other businesses. For the display in image **B**, the artist used neon lights to create a work of **neon art**. Point out the repeated shapes of the neon lights shown in image **B**. Where did the artist use line and color to add variety to this artwork?

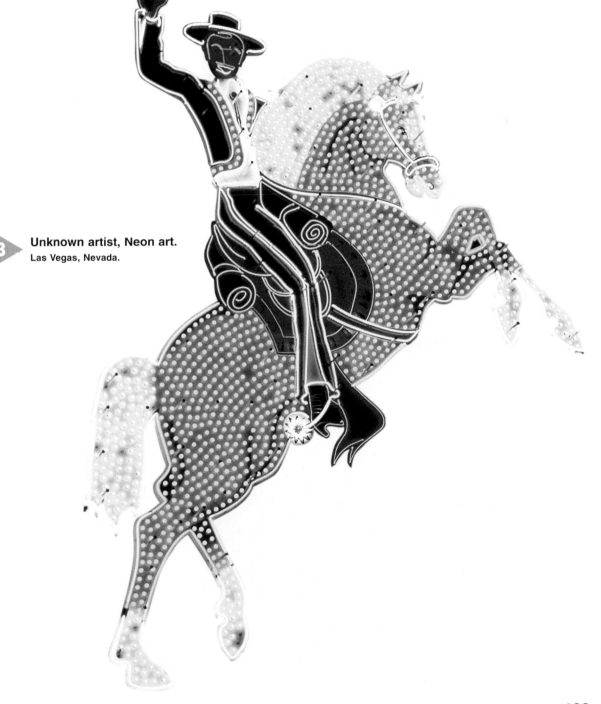

B **Unknown artist, Neon art.**
Las Vegas, Nevada.

Fiber Art

The artwork in image **C** is an example of **fiber art**, which is art made from plant fibers, yarn, or cloth. Fibers are commonly used to make everyday items, such as baskets, rugs, or clothing. The fibers in image **C** were used to create an abstract artwork.

How did the artist use line and color to create rhythm in this artwork? Where did the artist add variety?

Claire Zeisler, *Tri-Color Arch,* 1983–1984, fiber construction of hemp and synthetic fiber, 74 in. high. Metropolitan Museum of Art, New York, New York.

Think Critically

1. **Focus Skill** *READING SKILL* Explain in your own words how artists use everyday materials in unexpected ways. **SUMMARIZE AND PARAPHRASE**

2. What kinds of unusual materials would you like to use in an artwork?

3. **WRITE** Describe how to make an artwork using the unusual materials you listed for question 2.

Artist's Workshop

Create a Fiber Sculpture

MATERIALS

- string, yarn, cloth, pipe cleaners
- materials for armature
- pencil
- sketchbook
- glue

PLAN

Collect pieces of string, yarn, and cloth. Think of ways you can use these materials to create rhythm and variety in a fiber sculpture.

CREATE

1. Use cardboard tubes and foam trays to build an armature, or support structure, for your sculpture.

2. Sketch some ideas of the sculpture you want to create with the fibers you collected.

3. Twist, weave, tie, or drape the fibers on the armature. Glue where necessary.

REFLECT

Where in your sculpture did you create rhythm? Where did you add variety?

Safety Tips Ask your teacher to help you cut or bend pieces of wire for your armature.

JESÚS MOROLES

How did a man from a small Texas town become a world-famous sculptor?

 Jesús Moroles in his studio

For as long as he can remember, Jesús Moroles (hay•SOOS moh•ROH•lays) wanted to be a famous artist. Moroles's parents, both Mexican Americans, always supported him in his art training. Even though the family lived far away from the world's famous art centers, they encouraged their son to dream big. People looking at Moroles's artworks today can see two great influences—his Texas upbringing and his Mexican American heritage.

Jesús Moroles was born in 1950. After serving in the Air Force and completing college, he studied with another Texas sculptor, Luis Jiménez. Like Jiménez, who sculpted with fiberglass, Moroles chose to sculpt with another unusual material, granite.

 Jesús Moroles,
Houston Police Officers Memorial
1992, Texas granite, earth, grass, and water, 23 ft. x 120 ft. x 120 ft. Houston, Texas.

Moroles traveled to Carrara, Italy, to learn to work with marble. He practiced his art in the same marble quarry where the great Michelangelo had learned to sculpt 500 years before. Moroles then applied what he learned about marble to granite, a much harder and shinier type of stone.

Moroles sculpts granite with a wide variety of instruments, including power drills, diamond saws, and hand chisels. His mastery over this stone has led to many commissions for public sculptures, which he does in addition to his own artworks. Jesús Moroles's ability to "tear granite" into powerful and moving artworks has made him well-known and respected around the world.

Jesús Moroles, *Spirit Columns,*
1995, Texas red granite, 16 ft. x 15 ft. 3 in. x 14 ft. 3 in. Woodlands, Texas.

THINK ABOUT ART

The Houston Police Officers Memorial is made of Texas granite. How would the effect of the artwork change if it were made of white marble?

Multimedia Biographies
Visit *The Learning Site*
www.harcourtschool.com

Pop Art

In the 1960s and 1970s, Pop artists used bright, primary colors and showed familiar household objects in their art. They wanted to create art that all people could understand and enjoy. Describe the common objects you see in image **A**.

The artwork in image **A** is a painted bronze sculpture. How did the artist make a three-dimensional sculpture look like a two-dimensional painting?

Comic Book Style

Pop artists often copied the style of art they saw in advertisements, magazines, and other printed materials. Look at the pattern of diagonal lines in image **A**. Patterns of lines or dots, called **benday patterns**, are often used in comic books.

How does the benday pattern in this artwork create rhythm? Which elements of art add variety to the artwork?

A **Roy Lichtenstein,** *Picture and Pitcher,*
1978, painted bronze, 95 in. × 40 in. × 24 in.
Albright-Knox Art Gallery, Buffalo, New York.

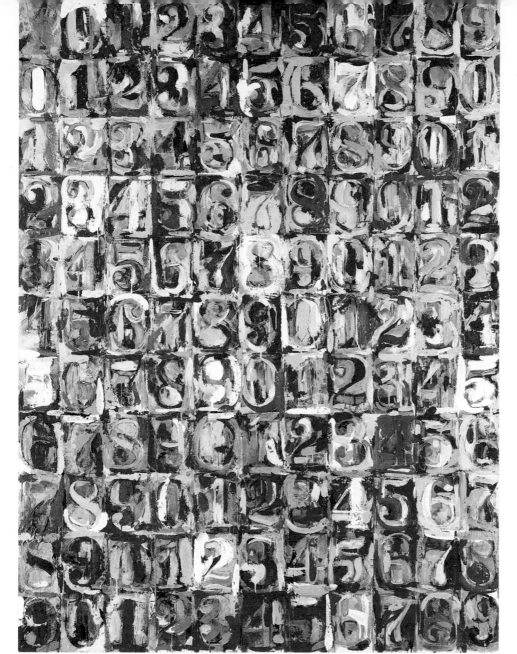

Jasper Johns,
Numbers in Color,
1958–1959, encaustic
and newspaper on
canvas, 66 in. × 49 in.
Albright-Knox Art
Gallery, Buffalo,
New York.

Everyday Symbols

Some Pop artists used common symbols, such as numbers and letters, in their artworks. Look at image **B**. Do you think the artist wanted the numbers to represent amounts, or did he use them simply as shapes? How did he arrange those shapes to create rhythm in this artwork? How did he add variety to keep the arrangement interesting?

Describe the color scheme in image **B**. How did the artist use color to create rhythm in this painting?

Math Link

Our numbers, which we call Arabic, actually came from India. Mathematicians in that country were the first to describe the concept of zero. They created the zero-to-nine numbering system in the seventh century. It was introduced to the Arab world in the eighth century.

Now look at the painting in image **C**. Do the letters have meaning, or do you think the artist used them only as shapes? How did the artist use color to create rhythm in this artwork? Where did he use shape to add variety?

The Pop Art painting in image **C** became a popular art print. **Art prints** are low-cost printed copies of original artworks. Today, most art prints are made by photographing the original artwork. In the past, prints were often made by **engraving**, or carving, the lines of an artwork into a block or a metal plate. The block or plate was covered with ink and pressed onto paper. Some artists still use this process to make prints.

 Robert Indiana, *The Great American Love,*
1972, oil on canvas, 144 in. × 144 in., 4 panels
each 72 in. × 72 in. Morgan Art Foundation.

Think Critically

1. **Focus Skill** *READING SKILL* In your own words, describe how Pop artists helped more people enjoy art. **SUMMARIZE AND PARAPHRASE**

2. How did new printing processes help the Pop Art movement?

3. **WRITE** Write a composition to compare and contrast the color schemes in images **B** and **C**.

Artist's Workshop

Create a Pop Art Painting

MATERIALS

- white paper
- scissors
- pencil
- tempera paints
- paint brushes
- paper plate
- water bowl

PLAN

Choose four numbers you would like to use as subjects in a Pop Art painting. Think of ways you can create rhythm and variety in your painting.

CREATE

1. Cut a piece of paper in half lengthwise. Divide it into four equal sections. Sketch a number in each section.

2. Paint three of your sections with tints and shades of the same color to create rhythm.

3. Add variety by using a different color in the fourth section.

REFLECT

Describe the color scheme you used.

Quick Tip

Primary or complementary color schemes are often used in Pop Art paintings.

Op Art

In the 1950s and 1960s, a group of artists created abstract paintings designed to "fool the eye." They used techniques such as linear perspective to create **optical illusions**, or false appearances, in their paintings. This new kind of art was called **Op Art**.

When linear perspective is used in a realistic painting, converging lines create the illusion of depth in a scene. In abstract paintings, converging lines create a sense of depth on the surface of the painting itself. Look at the Op Art painting in image **A**. Point to the place where the surface seems to bend away from you. Notice how the rows of dots converge, or get closer together, in the middle. How did the artist also use proportion to create this optical illusion?

 A   **Bridget Riley, *Fission,*** 1963, tempera on composition board, 35 in. × 34 in. The Museum of Modern Art, New York, New York.

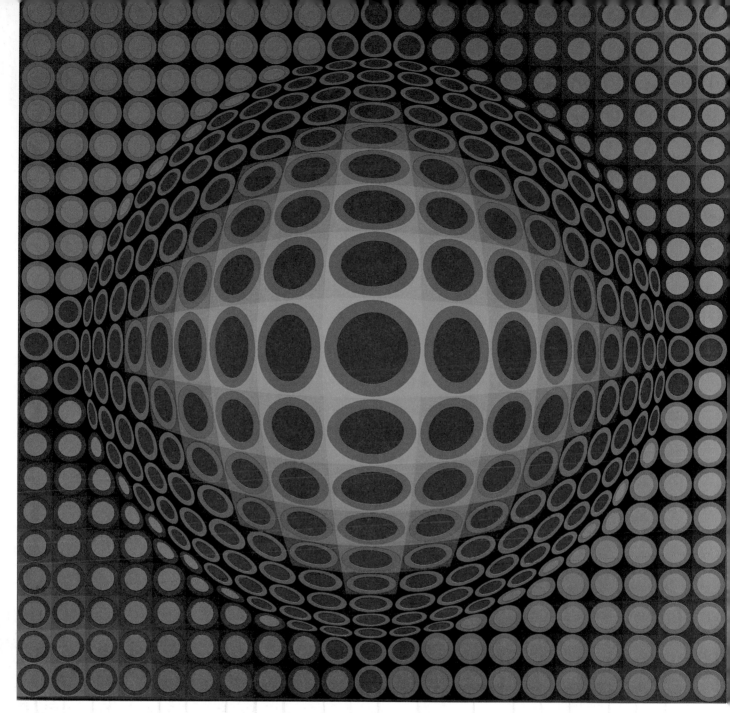

Victor Vasarely,
Vega 200,
1968, acrylic on canvas,
200 cm × 200 cm.

In image **B** the surface of the painting seems to bulge outward in the shape of a sphere. Notice the size of the center circle. Compare it to other circles in the same row. As the circles get smaller in proportion to each other, the sides of the sphere seem to move into the distance. How do artists use proportion to create a sense of distance in realistic paintings?

Where did the artist of image **B** create rhythm with equal-size circles? Where did he begin to vary the size of the circles?

Look at the design on the left side of image C. What part of the design seems closer to you, the center or the outer edge? Notice the amount of contrast, or difference, between the black and white lines in this design. Contrast creates emphasis. It makes the outer edge seem closer to the viewer.

Now look at the right side of image C. The black and white lines make the center of this design seem closer to the viewer, and the sides seem farther away.

 Frank Stella, *Paradoxe sur le Comedien,*
1974, synthetic polymer paint on canvas, 142 in. × 284 in.
Collection of the artist.

Think Critically

1. **READING SKILL** Summarize in two sentences how the artist used rhythm and variety in image B. **SUMMARIZE AND PARAPHRASE**

2. If the pattern in image A were made with tiny squares instead of dots, would the optical illusion be the same? Why?

3. **WRITE** Describe how you would use colors in image A to strengthen the optical illusion.

Artist's Workshop

Create an Optical Illusion

MATERIALS

- white paper
- pencil
- ruler
- colored marker

PLAN

Think of a way you can use lines of various sizes to create a design that contains an optical illusion.

CREATE

1. Use a pencil and ruler to draw parallel lines across your paper. At the top and bottom of the page, draw thick lines of equal width. Leave equal-sized spaces between them.

2. Moving toward the center of the page, draw gradually thinner lines with smaller spaces between them. The surface of your paper will appear to dip in the center.

3. Use a colored marker to darken and fill in your lines.

REFLECT

Which lines in your artwork create rhythm? Which lines add variety?

Quick Tip

You can work with your paper in a horizontal position or in a vertical position.

Fractal Art

How can mathematics be useful in art?

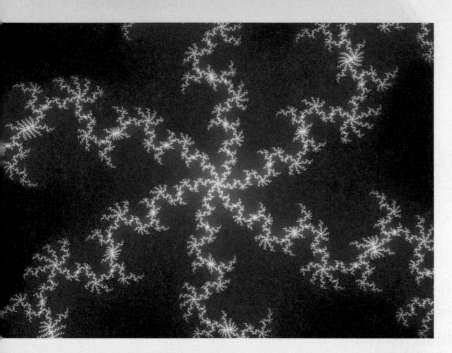

The fractal designs on these pages are artworks made with math. A fractal is a complicated shape based on a mathematical formula. When the formula is repeated, the shape becomes more and more complex. Snowflakes are fractal shapes based on the formula for a triangle.

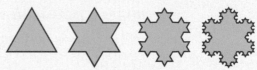

Artists today use computers to create complex fractal designs. Computers can quickly repeat the formula for a triangle, a curve, or a spiral thousands of times. Different colors and textures are assigned to the numbers in the formula, and as the computer repeatedly works the problem, beautiful shapes appear on the computer screen.

DID YOU KNOW?

Architects used mathematical formulas to create beautiful designs hundreds of years before computers were invented. This fractal design on the ceiling of a Los Angeles theater is based on the formula for an octagon.

Ceiling of Pantages Theatre, 1929. Hollywood, California.

Think About Art

What does each fractal design on these pages remind you of?

197

Technology and Art

Artists look for new ways to express themselves with materials, methods, and technologies. Today many artists use computers to create **computer-generated art**. Image **A** is a printed copy of a **digital image**, an image composed entirely of electronic bits of information.

Digital Texture

Look at the computer-generated textures on the left below. The artist of image **A** chose them from a CD-ROM library of visual textures, and applied them to different areas of his artwork. Point out where in the artwork each texture is used.

computer-
generated
textures

 Bob Rak, Illustration for children's book,
1999, digital image, 1,500 × 2,000 pixels. Collection of the artist.

198

Ronald Davis, *Ball and Chain,*
2001, digital print, 18 in. × 26 in,
Collection of the artist.

Digital Shading

The computer artist who created image **B** used the same
technique of shading that painters use to make objects look
three-dimensional. He chose tints and shades from a palette
(PA•luht), or selection, of computer-generated colors, and used
them to show light and shadows.

Highlights are the brightest spots on a surface where light
directly strikes an object. Look at the surface of the ball in
image **B**. How many lights seem to be shining on it? How did
the artist change the value of the pink color to show where the
lights strike the ball? Now look at the background. Where are
the shadows cast by the ball and chain? How did the artist
change the value of the purple color to show the shadows?

Large computers have been in use since the 1940s. The small personal computer, however, was not used in the United States until the 1970s. By 1985 the personal computer had become a common sight in American schools, homes, and offices.

Computer Art Programs

Image **C** was made with a computer art program. Computer software provided the shapes and colors, but the artist decided which ones to use and arranged them to make this composition. What kind of shape is repeated, in different sizes, in this artwork? What has the artist done to add variety to this composition?

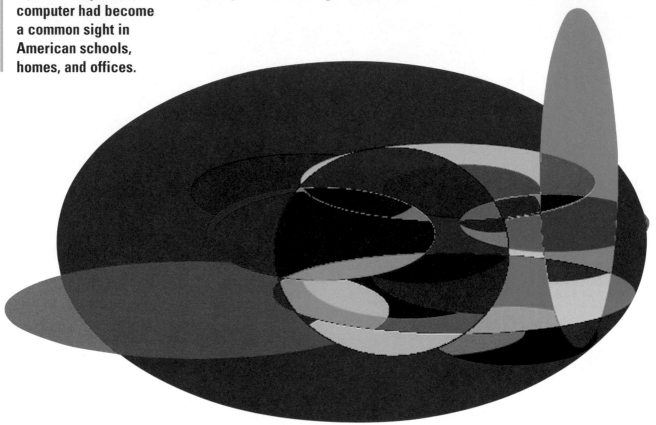

 Michael, age 10, *Colors and Shapes.*

Think Critically

1. **READING SKILL** Explain in your own words how the artist made objects in image **B** look real. **SUMMARIZE AND PARAPHRASE**

2. Identify the shadows in image **A**.

3. **WRITE** Write a short story using the characters and setting in image **A**.

Artist's Workshop

Create a Computer-Generated Design

MATERIALS

- computer
- word-processing program
- color printer

PLAN

Imagine an artwork you can create with computer-generated shapes. Think of ways you can create rhythm and variety in your computer-generated design.

CREATE

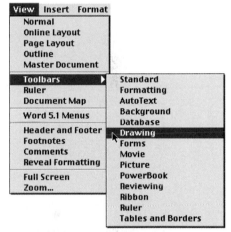

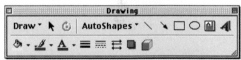

1. From the View menu of a computer, select Toolbars and then Drawing. Choose the basic shapes for your design, such as ovals, circles, rectangles, and squares.

2. Select the colors you want to use.

3. Arrange the shapes and colors into a composition that shows rhythm and variety.

REFLECT

Point out the shapes and colors that create rhythm in your design. Which shapes and colors did you use to add variety?

Quick Tip

You may want to add lines to your composition.

201

Unit 6 Review and Reflect

Vocabulary and Concepts

Choose the letter of the word or phrase that best completes each sentence.

1 ___ is created in an artwork by regular repetition of elements.

   A Color   **C** Rhythm

   B Variety   **D** Shape

2 ___ is a colored powder.

   F Neon   **H** Fiber

   G Pigment   **J** Canvas

3 Common objects are often shown in ___ artworks.

   A fiber   **C** Pop

   B neon   **D** Op

4 The false appearance of depth in an artwork is an optical ___.

   F print   **H** form

   G engraving   **J** illusion

5 ___ are the brightest spots on a surface that reflect the most light.

   A Textures   **C** Highlights

   B Illusions   **D** Benday patterns

Summarize and Paraphrase

Reread the two paragraphs of information on page 196. Use a chart to summarize and paraphrase the information.

Important Idea:	Important Idea:
Summary:	
Paraphrase:	

Write About Art

Write a summary of the artwork on page 198. Then use different words to write a paraphrase of your summary. Use the chart to plan your writing.

REMEMBER — YOU SHOULD

- describe the important parts of the artwork in your summary.

- use different words to restate the information in your paraphrase.

- use correct grammar, spelling, and punctuation.

Critic's Corner

Look at this artwork by Alexander Calder to answer the questions below.

DESCRIBE Would you describe the artwork as realistic or abstract? Why?

ANALYZE How did the artist create rhythm in his artwork? Where did he add variety?

INTERPRET What ideas do you think the artist wanted to communicate?

EVALUATE Did the artist successfully communicate his ideas?

Alexander Calder, Untitled,
1971, gouache on paper, $43\frac{1}{2}$ in. × $29\frac{1}{2}$ in.
Private collection.

Student Handbook

C O N T E N T S

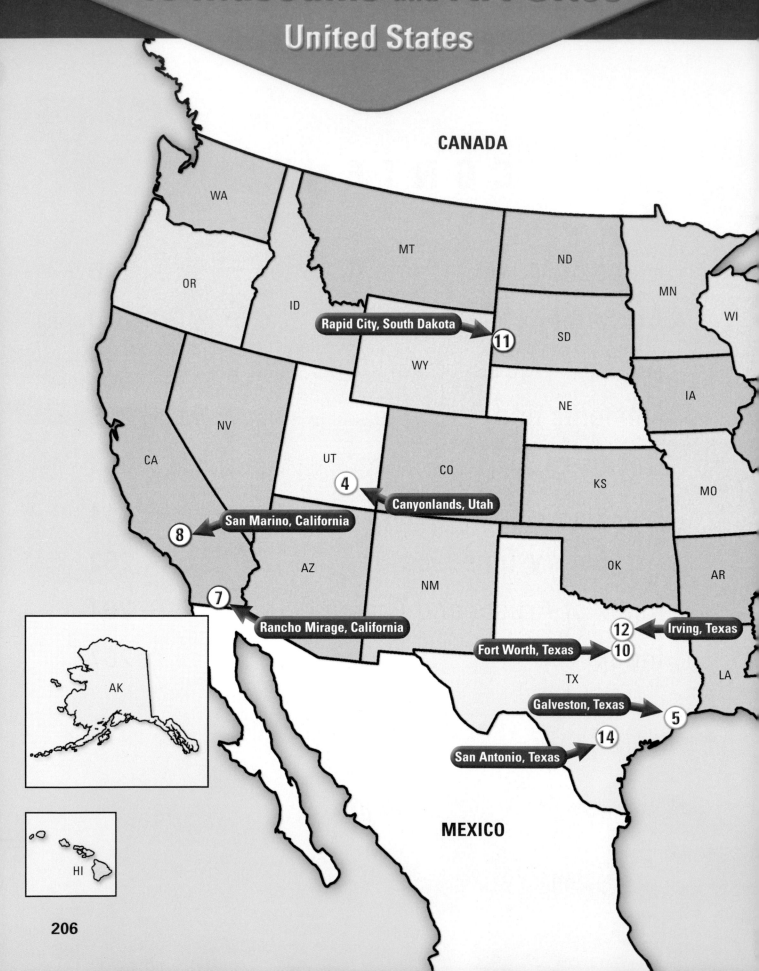

15 Museums and Art Sites
United States

CANADA

Rapid City, South Dakota → 11

Canyonlands, Utah → 4

San Marino, California → 8

Rancho Mirage, California → 7

Irving, Texas → 12

Fort Worth, Texas → 10

Galveston, Texas → 5

San Antonio, Texas → 14

WA
OR
ID
MT
ND
MN
WI
NV
UT
WY
SD
NE
IA
CA
CO
KS
MO
AZ
NM
OK
AR
TX
LA
AK
HI

MEXICO

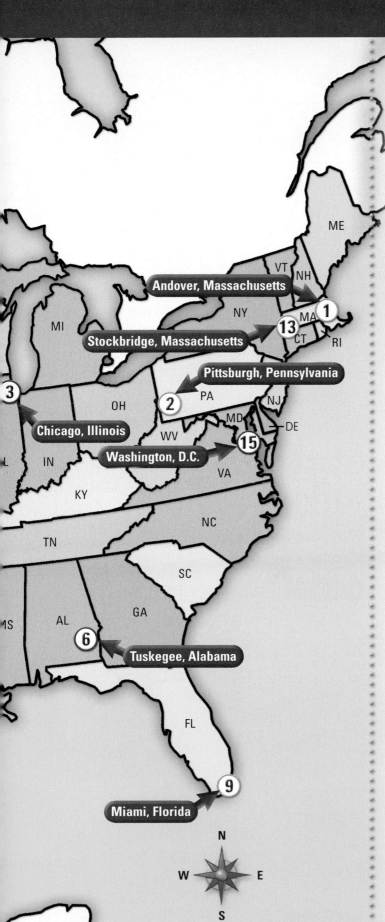

LOCATE IT

See art for these sites on the pages shown.

Andover, Massachusetts

Stockbridge, Massachusetts

Pittsburgh, Pennsylvania

Chicago, Illinois

Washington, D.C.

Tuskegee, Alabama

Miami, Florida

Use the Electronic Art Gallery CD-ROM, Intermediate, to locate artworks from other museums and art sites.

15 Museums and Art Sites
World

NORTH AMERICA

Amsterdam, Netherlands ➡ 14

Munich, Germany

EUROPE

2 ⬅ Toronto, Canada

Paris, France ➡ 9

10

7 ⬅ Vienna, Austria

13 ⬅ Washington, D.C.

3 ⬅ Sicily, Italy

12 ⬅ Mexico

AFRICA

Central America ➡ 8

4 5 Nigeria

Ivory Coast ➡ 4

6 ⬅ Brazil

SOUTH AMERICA

N
W E
S

ANTARCTICA

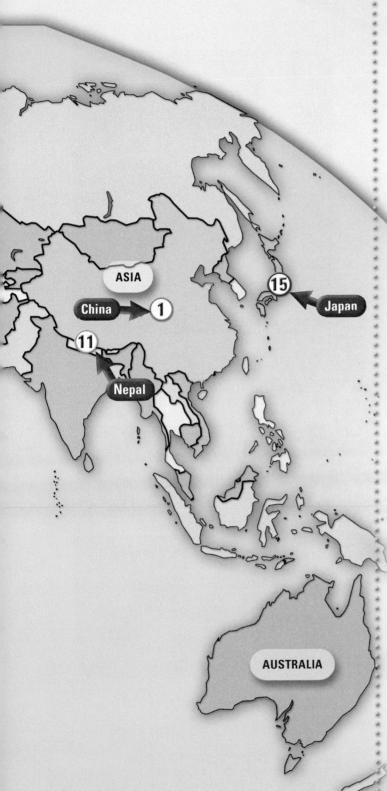

See art for these sites on the pages shown.

Art Safety

Listen carefully when your teacher explains how to use art materials.

Read the labels on materials before you use them.

Tell your teacher if you have allergies.

Wear a smock or apron to keep your clothes clean.

Use tools carefully. Hold sharp objects so that they cannot hurt you or others. Wear safety glasses to protect your eyes.

Use the kind of markers and inks that will not stain your clothes.

Clean up spills right away so no one will slip and fall.

Always wash your hands after using art materials.

Show respect for other students. Walk carefully around their work. Never touch classmates' work without asking first.

Cover your skin if you have a cut or scratch.

Art Techniques

Trying Ways to Draw

There are lots of ways to draw. You can sketch quickly to show a rough idea of your subject, or you can draw carefully to show just how it looks to you. Try to draw every day. Keep your drawings in your sketchbook so you can see how your drawing skills improve.

Here are some ideas for drawing. To start, get out some pencils and either your sketchbook or a sheet of paper.

GESTURE DRAWING

Gesture drawings are quick sketches that are made with loose arm movements. The gesture drawing on the left shows a rough idea of what a baseball player looks like. The more careful drawing on the right shows details of the player's uniform and face. ▶

◀ **Find some photographs of people or animals.** Make gesture drawings of them. Draw quickly. Don't try to show details.

◀ **Ask a friend to pose for a gesture drawing.** Take no more than two or three minutes to finish your sketch.

212

CONTOUR DRAWING

Contour drawings show only the outlines of the shapes that make up objects. They do not show the objects' color or shading. The lines that go around shapes are called **contour lines.** Use your finger to trace around the contour lines of the truck in this picture. Trace the lines around each of the shapes that make up the truck.

◀ **A blind contour drawing is made without looking at your paper as you draw.** Choose a simple object to draw, like a leaf. Pick a point on the object where you will begin drawing. Move your eyes slowly around the edge of the object. Without looking at your paper, move your pencil in the same way that your eyes move. Your first drawings may not look like the object you are looking at. Practice with different objects to improve your skill.

Continuous contour drawings are made without ▶ lifting your pencil off the paper. Draw something simple, like a chair. Look back and forth between the object and your paper. You will have to go over some lines more than once to keep from lifting your pencil off the paper.

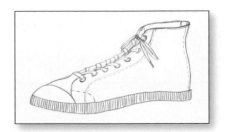

◀ **Now try making a contour drawing of another object, such as a shoe.** Look at your paper and lift your pencil whenever you want to. Then add details.

TONAL DRAWING

Tonal drawings show the dark and light areas of objects using tones, or shades, of one color. They do not include contour lines. Look at the photograph at the right. Notice which areas are dark and which are light. Now look at the tonal drawing. Even without contour lines, you can tell what the drawing shows. ▶

◀ **Experiment with your pencils.** You can use **cross-hatching,** or a pattern of crossed lines, to show dark areas in a tonal drawing. Try smudging some of the lines together with your fingers. To darken large areas, use the flat edge of a dull pencil point. Use an eraser to lighten some of your marks.

Try a tonal drawing of a simple object ▶ **like a spoon.** Look at the object closely. Do not draw contour lines. Notice the shapes of the dark and light areas on the object. Use the edge of your pencil point to copy the dark shapes. Use cross-hatching in some areas. Use an eraser to lighten marks where needed.

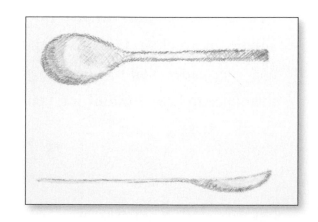

CONTOURS AND TONES

Try combining tonal drawing with contour drawing. Start by making a tonal drawing of something with an interesting shape, like a backpack. Look at it carefully to see the tones of dark and light. ▶

Then look at the object again to see its contours. Draw contour lines around the shapes that make up the object. ▶

You might prefer to start with a contour drawing. Be sure you draw the outline of each shape in the object. Then add tones with shading or cross-hatching. ▼

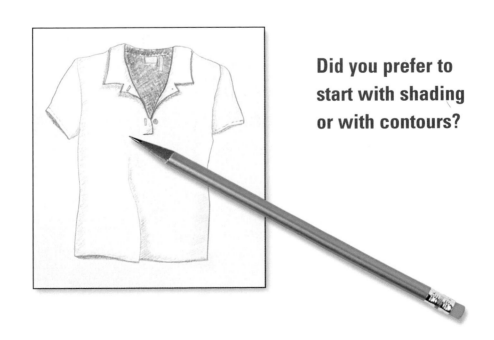

Did you prefer to start with shading or with contours?

Art Techniques

Experimenting with Paint

Working with colors is always fun. Experimenting with paint will help you learn about color and how you can use it in your artwork.

These are some things you should have when you paint: old newspapers to cover your work area, an old shirt to cover your clothes, tempera paints or watercolors, plastic plates or plastic egg cartons for mixing paint, paper, paintbrushes, a jar or bowl of water, and paper towels.

TEMPERA PAINTS

Tempera paints are water-based, so they are easy to clean up. The colors are bright and easy to mix.

GETTING STARTED

Start experimenting with different kinds of brushstrokes.
Try painting with lots of paint on the brush and then with the brush almost dry. (You can dry the paintbrush by wiping it across a paper towel.) Make a brushstroke by twisting the paintbrush on your paper. See how many different brushstrokes you can make by rolling, pressing, or dabbing the brush on the paper.

Now load your brush with as much paint as it will ▶ hold, and make a heavy brushstroke. Use a craft stick or another tool to draw a pattern in it.

Use what you've learned to paint a picture.
Use as many different brushstrokes as you can. ▶

MIXING COLORS

Even if you have only a few colors of tempera paint, you can mix them to make almost any color you want. Use the **primary colors** red, yellow, and blue to create the **secondary colors** orange, green, and violet.

◀ **Mix dark and light colors.** To make darker colors (**shades**), add black. To make lighter colors (**tints**), add white. See how many shades and tints of a single color you can make.

TECHNIQUES TO TRY

Pointillism is a technique that makes the viewer's eyes mix the colors. Use colors, such as blue and yellow, that make a third color when mixed. Make small dots of color close together without letting the dots touch. In some areas, place the two different colors very close together. Stand back from your paper. What happens to the colors as your eyes "mix" them? ▶

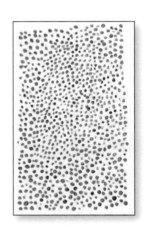

◀ **Impasto is a technique that creates a thick or bumpy surface on a painting.** You can create an impasto painting by building up layers of paint, or by thickening your paint with a material such as wheat paste. Mix some paint and wheat paste in a small bowl. Spread some of the mixture on a piece of cardboard. Experiment with tools such as a toothpick, a plastic fork, or a comb to make textures in the impasto. Mix more colors and use them to make an impasto picture or design.

217

Art Techniques

WATERCOLORS

Watercolors usually come in little dry cakes. You have to add the water! So keep a jar of clean water and some paper towels nearby as you paint. Use paper that is made for watercolors.

GETTING STARTED

Dip your paintbrush in water and then dab it on one of the watercolors. Try a brushstroke. Watercolors are transparent. Since you can see through them, the color on your paper will never be as dark as the color of the cake. Use different amounts of water. What happens to the color when you use a lot of water?

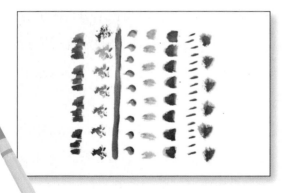

Now rinse your brush in water and use another color. Try different kinds of brushstrokes—thick and thin, squiggles and waves, dots and blobs. Change colors often.

Try using one color on top of a different color that is already dry. Work quickly. If your brushstrokes are too slow, the dry color underneath can become dull. If you want part of your painting to be white, don't paint that part. The white comes from the color of the paper.

MIXING COLORS

Experiment with mixing watercolors right on your paper. Try painting with a very wet brush. Add a wet color on top of, or just touching, another wet color. Try three colors together. ▶

You can also mix colors on your paintbrush. Dip your brush into one color and then another before you paint. Try it with green and yellow. Clean your paintbrush and try some other combinations. To clean any paint cakes that you have used for mixing, just wipe them with a paper towel. ▶

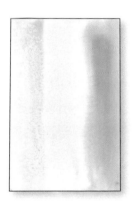

TECHNIQUES TO TRY

◀ **Try making a watercolor wash.** Start with a patch of dark green. Then clean your paintbrush and get it very wet. Use it to "wash" the color down the page. (You can also do this with a foam brush or a sponge.)

You can wet all of one side of the paper, brush a stroke of color across it, and let the color spread. Try two or three color washes together. For a special effect, sprinkle salt onto the wet paper.

Try using tempera paints and watercolors together. ▶ Start with a two-color watercolor wash. Let it dry. Then use several kinds of brushstrokes to paint a design on top of the wash with tempera paint.

Remember these techniques when you paint designs or pictures. Be sure to clean your paintbrushes and work area when you have finished.

Working with Clay

Clay is a special kind of mud or earth that holds together and is easy to shape when it is mixed with water. Clay objects can be fired, or heated at a high temperature, to make them harden. They can also be left in the air to dry until hard.

To make an object with clay, work on a clean, dry surface. (A brown paper bag makes a good work surface.) Have some water handy. If the clay starts to dry out, add a few drops of water at a time. When you are not working with the clay, store it in a plastic bag to keep it moist.

▲

You can use an assortment of tools. Use a rolling pin to make flat slabs of clay. Use a plastic knife or fork, keys, a comb, or a pencil to add texture or designs to the objects you make out of clay.

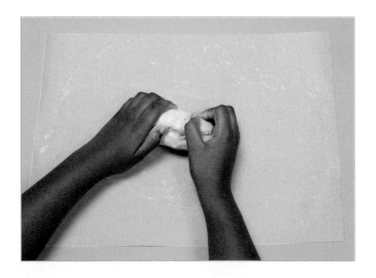

▲

Start working with a piece of clay by making sure it has no air bubbles in it. Press it down, fold it over, and press it down again. This process is called **kneading**.

MODELING

Try making different forms with your ▶
clay. If one of your forms reminds you of an
animal or a person, continue to mold the form
by pinching and pulling the clay.

◀ **You can join two pieces of clay**
together. Carve small lines on the edges
that will be joined. This is called **scoring**.
Then use **slip,** or clay dissolved in water,
to wet the surfaces. Press the pieces
together and smooth the seams.

To make a bigger form,
wrap a slab of clay
around a tube or
crumpled newspaper.

Try adding patterns, textures, or details to your form.
Experiment with your tools. Press textured objects into
the clay and lift them off. Brush a key across the clay.
Press textured material like burlap into your clay, lift it
off, and add designs. If you change your mind, smooth the
clay with your fingers and try something else.

Art Techniques

USING SLABS

Roll your clay out flat, to between $\frac{1}{4}$ inch and $\frac{1}{2}$ inch thick. Shape the clay by molding it over something like a bowl or crumpled paper. ▶

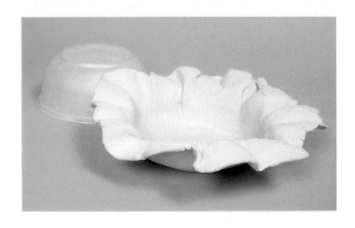

◀ **To make a slab box, roll your clay out flat.** Use a plastic knife to cut six equal-sized squares or rectangles for the bottom, top, and sides of your box. Score the edges, and then let the pieces dry until they feel like leather.

Join the pieces together with slip. ▶ Then smooth the seams with your fingers.

USING COILS

To make a coil pot, roll pieces of clay against a hard surface. Use your whole hand to make long clay ropes. ▶

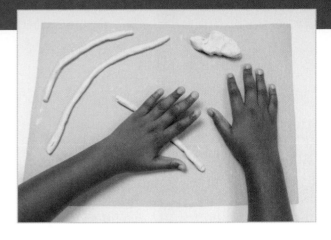

◀ **Make the bottom of your pot by coiling a clay rope into a circle.** Smooth the seams with your fingers. To build the sides, attach coils of clay on top of one another. Score and wet the pieces with slip as you attach them. Smooth the inside as you work. You may smooth the outside or let the coils show.

MAKING A CLAY RELIEF ▶

A relief is a sculpture raised from a surface. To make a relief, draw a simple design on a slab of clay. Roll some very thin ropes and attach them to the lines of the design. This is called the **additive method** because you are adding clay to the slab.

◀ **You can also make a relief sculpture by carving a design out of your clay slab.** This is called the **subtractive method** because you are taking away, or subtracting, clay from the slab.

223

Art Techniques

Exploring Printmaking

When you make a print, you transfer color from one object to another. If you have ever left a muddy footprint on a clean floor, you know what a print is. Here are some printmaking ideas to try.

COLLOGRAPH PRINTS

A **collograph** is a combination of a **collage** and a **print**. To make a collograph, you will need cardboard, glue, paper, newspapers, a brayer (a roller for printing), printing ink or paint, a flat tray such as a foam food tray, and some paper towels or sponges. You will also need some flat objects to include in the collage. Try things like old keys, string, lace, paper clips, buttons, small shells, or burlap.

Arrange objects on the cardboard ▶ in a pleasing design. Glue the objects to the surface, and let the glue dry.

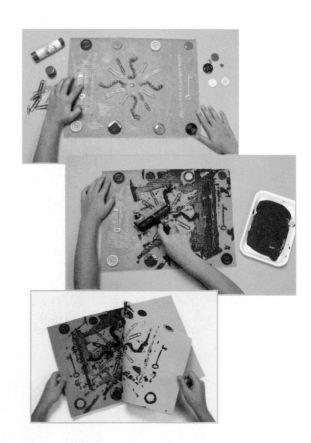

Prepare your ink while the collage ▶ is drying. Place a small amount of ink or paint on your foam tray. Roll the brayer through the ink until it is evenly coated. Gently run the brayer over the collage. Most of the ink should be on the objects.

Now press a piece of paper onto ▶ the inked collage. Gently rub the paper. Peel off the paper and let the ink dry. You've made a collograph!

224

MULTICOLOR PRINTS

You can use different colors of tempera paint to make a multicolor print with repeated shapes. You will need poster board or a foam tray (such as a food tray), cardboard, scissors, glue, paper, water, tempera paint, and a paintbrush.

First cut out some interesting shapes from the poster board or foam tray. Carve or poke holes and lines into the shapes. ▶

Arrange the shapes on the cardboard to make an interesting design. Glue down the pieces. When the glue is dry, paint the shapes with different colors of tempera paint. Try not to get paint on the cardboard. ▶

◀ **While the paint is wet, place a sheet of paper on top of your design.** Gently rub the paper, and peel it off carefully. Let the paint dry.

After the shapes dry, paint them again with different colors. Print the same paper again, but turn it so that the designs and colors overlap.

Try using different colors, paper, and objects to make prints.

225

Displaying Your Artwork

Displaying your artwork is a good way to share it.
Here are some ways to make your artwork look its best.

DISPLAYING ART PRINTS

Select several pictures that go together well. Line them up along a wall or on the floor. Try grouping the pictures in different ways. Choose an arrangement that you like. Attach a strong string across a wall. Use clothespins or paper clips to hang your pictures on the string.

Make a frame. Use a piece of cardboard that is longer and wider than the art. In the center of the cardboard, draw a rectangle that is slightly smaller than your picture. Have an adult help you cut out the rectangle. Then decorate your frame. Choose colors and textures that look good with your picture. You can paint the frame or use a stamp to print a design on it. You can add texture by gluing strips of cardboard or rows of buttons onto your frame.

Mount your picture. Tape the corners of your artwork to the back of the frame. Cut a solid piece of cardboard the same size as the frame. Then glue the framed artwork to the cardboard. Tape a loop of thread on the back. Hang up your framed work.

DISPLAYING SCULPTURES

To display your clay objects or sculptures, find a location where your work will be safe from harm. Look for a display area where people won't bump into your exhibit or damage your work.

Select several clay objects or sculptures that go together well. Try grouping them in different ways. Place some of the smaller objects on boxes. When you find an arrangement that you like, remove your artworks, tape the boxes to the table, and drape a piece of cloth over the boxes. Pick a plain cloth that will look good under your artworks, try adding a few interesting folds in the cloth, and place your artworks back on the table.

Now invite your friends and family over to see your work!

227

Line

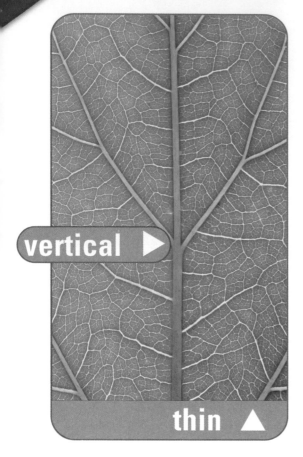

vertical ▶

thin ▲

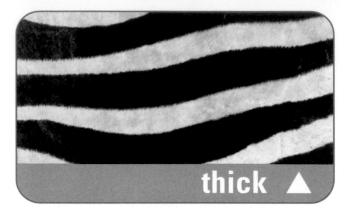

thick ▲

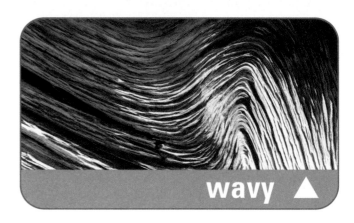

wavy ▲

straight ▼

horizontal ▲

zigzag ▼

Shape

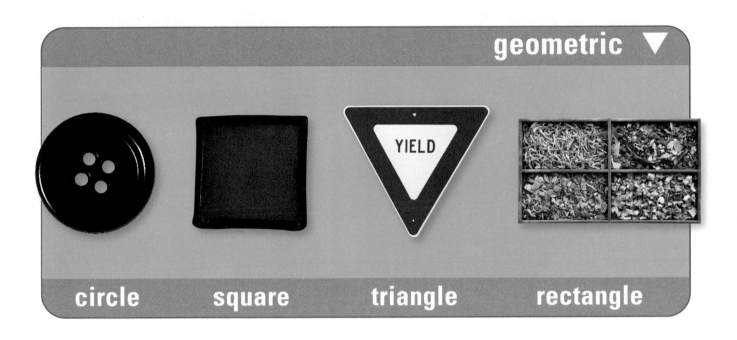

geometric ▼

circle square triangle rectangle

symbol ▲

▼ **organic**

Color and Value

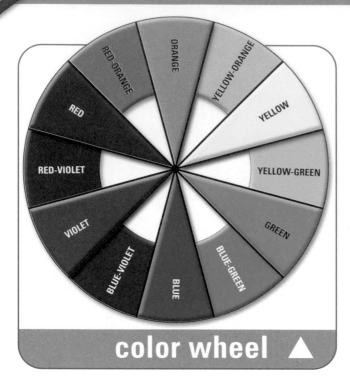

color wheel ▲

cool colors ▲

warm colors ▲

complementary colors ▲

▼ **value**

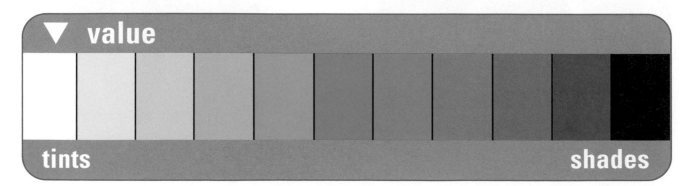

tints　　　　**shades**

Texture

bumpy ▲

▼ **soft**

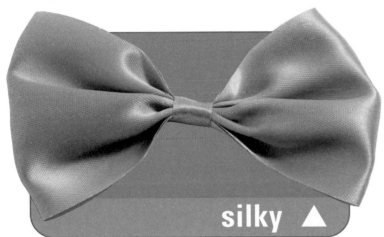

silky ▲

▼ **smooth**

rough ▲

Form

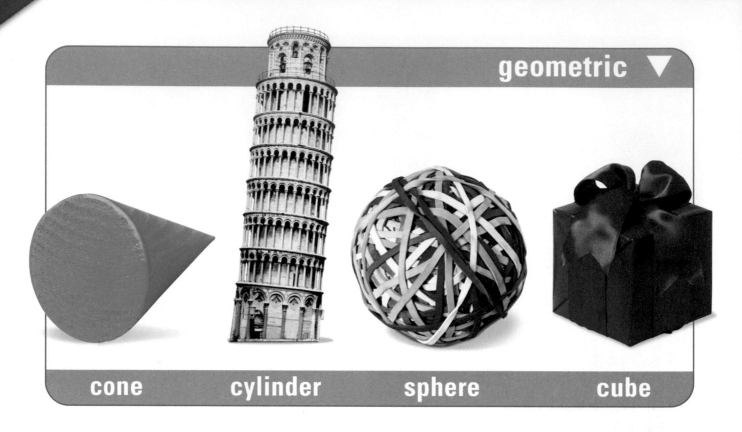

geometric ▼

| cone | cylinder | sphere | cube |

organic ▲

Space

overlapping ▼

atmospheric perspective ▼

background ▶

middle ground ▶

foreground ▶

positive ▶

◀ negative

▲ linear perspective

233

Pattern

234

Proportion

Emphasis

Balance

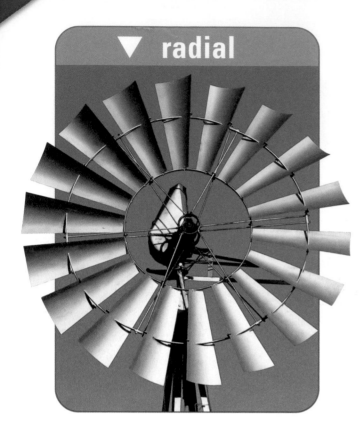

▼ radial

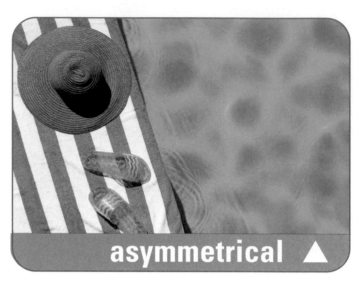

asymmetrical ▲

symmetrical ▲

Unity and Variety

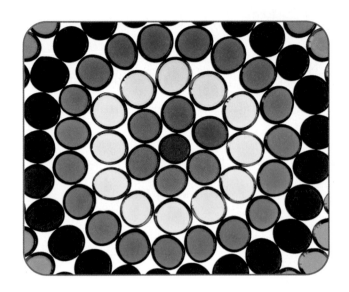

239

Gallery of Artists

Sofonisba Anguissola

(1532–1625) Italy, painter. Sofonisba Anguissola [soh•foh•NIS•bah ahn•GWEES•soh•lah] introduced new painting techniques. She painted portraits of the Spanish royal family. **pages 156–157**

Giuseppe Arcimboldo

(1527–1593) Italy, painter. Arcimboldo [ar•cheem•BOHL•doh] first worked for his father, supplying artworks for cathedrals. He became famous for his unusual portraits. **page 138**

John James Audubon

(1785–1851) France/ United States, painter. Audubon grew up in France, developing an interest in art and nature. After he moved to the United States, Audubon began painting American birds. **pages 106–107**

Romare Bearden

(1911–1988) United States, painter/ collage artist. Bearden often based his collages on his childhood memories and his love of jazz. **page 53**

Giovanni Lorenzo Bernini

(1598–1680) Italy, sculptor/painter/architect. Bernini [ber•NEE•nee] is known as the greatest artist of the Baroque era. He created life-size public sculptures, as well as fountains, tombs, and churches. **page 133**

Sandro Botticelli

(1445–1510) Italy, painter. Botticelli [bot•tee•CHEL•lee] painted elegant portraits, religious scenes, and illustrations of Greek and Roman legends. **page 158**

Anna Mary Richards Brewster

(1870–1952) United States, painter. Brewster learned to paint by watching her father, a famous painter of landscapes and seascapes. **page 94**

Jennie Augusta Brownscombe

(1850–1936) United States, painter. Brownscombe was born in Pennsylvania. She moved to New York City to study art. Her works often show highly detailed scenes from American history. **page 116**

Alexander Calder

(1898–1976) United States, painter/sculptor. Calder's mobiles, stabiles, and paintings can be found in museums around the world. **page 203**

Mary Cassatt

(1844–1926) United States and France, painter/printmaker. Cassatt [kuh•SAT] was born in the United States but spent most of her adult life in France. Her paintings were most often of human subjects, especially women and children. **page 124**

Emiliano di Cavalcanti

(1897–1976) Brazil, painter. Di Cavalcanti began his career by drawing caricatures for magazines and books. He borrowed ideas from a variety of art movements, such as Post-Impressionism, Expressionism, Cubism, and Surrealism. **page 100**

Paul Cézanne

(1839–1906) France, painter. When Cézanne [say•ZAHN] looked at nature, he saw geometric forms. His works were not understood at the time, but his ideas led to an art movement called Cubism. **pages 26, 60, 160**

Gallery of Artists

Dale Chihuly

(1941–) United States, glass artist. Dale Chihuly [chih•HOO•lee] is best known for his colorful, abstract glass works. One of his biggest projects is the 35-foot-high, 550-foot-long pedestrian bridge in Tacoma, Washington. **page 174**

Karl Ciesluk

(1950–) Canada, sculptor. Karl Ciesluck [SEE•zluk] grew up in Ontario, Canada. He attributes his interest in environmental art to his upbringing in a quiet, country setting. **page 109**

Leonardo da Vinci

(1452–1519) Italy, painter and sculptor. Da Vinci was responsible for some of the most influential images in art history, including the *Mona Lisa* and *The Last Supper*. His use of space, light, and shadows influenced later artists. **page 98**

Edgar Degas

(1834–1917) France, painter. Edgar Degas [duh•GAH] was fascinated by photographic techniques. In many of his paintings, he captured his subjects in a revealing moment, as if on film. Degas painted many pictures of ballet dancers, often in rehearsal or backstage. **page 162**

Robert Delaunay

(1885–1941) France, painter. Delaunay [duh•loh•NAY] is known as one of the earliest painters of abstract and nonrepresentational works. **page 168**

André Derain

(1880–1954) France, painter/sculptor/ illustrator. Derain helped found the art movement called Fauvism. He also became known for his book illustrations and his set designs for plays. **page 113**

Ed Dwight

(1933–) United States, sculptor. Dwight is the first African American trained to be an astronaut. He has created memorials to Dr. Martin Luther King, Jr., George Washington Carver, Harriet Tubman, and Frederick Douglass. **page 97**

M. C. Escher

(1898–1972) Holland, graphic artist. Escher [ESH•er] studied architecture before becoming an artist. He is known for his drawings that surprise viewers with optical illusions. **pages 63, 66–67**

Janet Fish

(1938–) United States, painter. Fish's realistic paintings show light reflected through glass, water, and mirrors. Fish always works on two paintings at the same time— one for cloudy days and one for sunny days. **pages 46–47**

Louise Freshman-Brown

page 169

Giambologna

(1529–1608) Flanders/Italy, sculptor. Giambologna [jahm•boh•LOH•nyah] studied Classical and Renaissance sculpture and became a court sculptor in Florence. He soon developed into one of the most influential sculptors in Europe. **page 108**

Robert Glen

(1940–) Kenya/United States, sculptor. Glen was born in Kenya, where he developed a strong interest in natural history and art. Glen began his sculpting career when he moved to the United States. His work can be found both in public spaces and in many private collections around the world. **page 54**

Andy Goldsworthy

(1956–) England, sculptor and land artist. Goldsworthy uses nature for both his materials and his settings. His sculptures are photographed the minute they are completed. **page 110**

Nancy Graves

(1940–1995) United States, sculptor/painter. Graves produced many painted bronze sculptures and abstract paintings that reflected her interest in the natural sciences. **page 73**

John Lawrence Groff

page 102

Duane Hanson

(1925–1996) United States, sculptor. Hanson was inspired by the Pop Art movement. Many of his later works were painted and clothed human figures made out of fiberglass and resin. **page 123**

Winslow Homer

(1836–1910) United States, painter/illustrator. Homer was fascinated by the ocean. He painted many works that show the coasts of Maine (where he lived), the Bahamas, Cuba, and Florida. Many of his works show humans struggling against powerful seas. **page 144**

Edward Hopper

(1882–1967) United States, painter. Hopper is best known for his realistic scenes of city streets, country roads, and buildings. His paintings often show sad, lonely people in their everyday lives. **page 164**

Robert Indiana

(1928–) United States, painter/sculptor/printmaker. Indiana is one of the central figures of American Pop Art. He transforms symbols found on signs and advertisements into brilliantly colored artworks. **page 190**

Jasper Johns

(1930–) United States, painter/printmaker/sculptor. Johns's works include a wide variety of media. He has created sculptures with objects such as flashlights, cans, and paintbrushes. **page 189**

Frida Kahlo

(1907–1954) Mexico, painter. Kahlo taught herself to paint after a disabling traffic accident. She was married to, and sometimes worked with, Mexican muralist Diego Rivera. **page 129**

Wassily Kandinsky

(1866–1944) Russia, painter/writer. Wassily Kandinsky [vuh•SEEL•yee kan•DIN•skee] was one of the pioneers of abstract art. His earlier works were expressive, colorful compositions that contained figures. His later works were less realistic. **page 59**

Anish Kapoor

(1954–) United Kingdom, sculptor. Kapoor's art reflects his Asian and European heritage. He has used wood, sandstone, slate, large blocks of stone, and metal in his artworks. **page 182**

Paul Klee

(1879–1940) Switzerland, painter. Klee's [KLAY] paintings, drawings, and etchings have been described as childlike. His parents were both musicians. Klee himself was a professional violinist before becoming an artist. **page 29**

Gallery of Artists

GG Kopilak

United States, painter. Kopilak is best known for hiding a self-portrait within her still-life compositions. She uses materials such as stone, fabric, glass, and paper in her compositions. **page 128**

Roy Lichtenstein

(1923–1997) United States, painter. Lichtenstein [LIK•tuhn•styn] was one of the best-known American painters in the Pop Art movement. His most famous paintings imitate comic strips. Lichtenstein painted the same patterns of lines and dots that comic books use, and he often included speech bubbles in his works. **pages 64, 188**

Jenne Magafan

(1916–1952) United States, painter. Magafan created uplifting murals during the hard times of the Great Depression. She often collaborated with her twin sister, Ethel. **page 114**

Kasimir Malevich

(1878–1935) Russia, painter. As a child, Kasimir Malevich [kuh•ZEE•mir muh•LAY•vich] taught himself how to paint. As an adult, he developed a form of abstract painting that used geometric shapes and white backgrounds. **page 139**

Edouard Manet

(1832–1883) France, painter and print-maker. Manet [ma•NAY] is known as a realistic painter, although he was influenced by the Impressionists of the 1870s. Manet helped introduce modern, urban subjects in paintings. **page 24**

Henri Matisse

(1869–1954) France, painter. Henri Matisse [ahn•REE mah•TEES] led a group of artists who used bright colors and strong brushstrokes. This was considered so shocking that the artists were known as the Fauves [FOHVZ], or "wild beasts." **page 150**

Gil Mayers

United States, painter/ printmaker. Mayers fell in love with art and jazz music in New York City. His work portrays the world of jazz and its musicians. **page 32**

Michelangelo

[my•kuhl•AN•juh•loh] (1475–1564) Italy, painter/sculptor. Michelangelo produced his first two sculptures by the age of sixteen. He went on to become one of the greatest Renaissance painters, sculptors, and architects. **page 132**

Claude Monet

(1840–1926) France, painter. Monet [moh•NAY], one of the founders of Impressionism, was not well accepted by the art world in his time. However, Monet is considered today to be a master artist. **page 78**

Roberto Montenegro

(1887–1968) Mexico, painter/printmaker/ illustrator. At the beginning of his career, Montenegro created magazine drawings and book illustrations. Later in life, he mastered the art of portrait painting. **page 123**

Jesús Moroles

(1950–) United States, sculptor. Jesús Moroles [hay•SOOS moh•ROH•lays] learned masonry, or stonecutting, from his uncle. Moroles chooses interesting pieces of granite from stone quarries. He works on about twenty pieces at a time. **pages 69, 186–187**

Gallery of Artists

Elizabeth Murray

(1940–) United States, painter/printmaker. Murray's earliest works were abstract. Her style changed when she created "shaped canvases," raised canvases with figures painted on them. **page 180**

Louise Nevelson

(about 1899–1988) Russia/United States, sculptor. Nevelson is well known for her large, assembled sculptures. Some of her assemblages take up whole walls or entire rooms. **page 178**

Elisabet Ney

(1833–1907) Germany/United States, sculptor. Ney was best known for her portrait sculptures. She began her career in 1867 as a court sculptor for King Ludwig II of Bavaria. Then she moved to the United States and created portraits of notable Americans. **page 137**

Georgia O'Keeffe

(1887–1986) United States, painter. O'Keeffe became one of the most important American artists of the early twentieth century. Many of her most famous paintings show close-up views of flowers. **page 37**

Claes Oldenburg

(1929–) Sweden, sculptor. Claes Oldenburg [KLAHS OHL•duhn•berg] is best known for his oversized sculptures of ordinary objects. He has created several large-scale public artworks. **pages 26, 179**

Julian Onderdonk

(1882–1922) United States, painter. Some of Onderdonk's favorite Texas subjects were sunlit fields of bluebonnets, cactuses in bloom, and dusty roads. **page 84**

Diana Ong

(1940–) United States, multimedia artist. Diana Ong works in several media including watercolors, acrylics, ceramics, and computer art. **page 33**

Nam June Paik

(1932–) Korea, composer/video artist. In the early 1960s, Paik was known as a composer of electronic music. In 1964, he moved to New York City, and began making video art and TV sculptures. **page 72**

Pablo Picasso

(1881–1973) Spain, painter. Picasso was one of the greatest artists of the twentieth century. He helped found an art movement called Cubism. Picasso was influenced by the style of African sculpture. **page 28**

Camille Pissarro

(1830–1903) France, painter/teacher. Camille Pissarro [ka•MEE pih•SAH•roh] was a leader in the Impressionist movement. Pissarro painted landscapes, river scenes, and street scenes of Paris and London. **page 89**

Robert Rauschenberg

(1925–) United States, painter/sculptor/printmaker. Rauschenberg [ROW•shuhn•berg] is a major artist in the Pop Art movement. He invented "combine painting," a combination of sculpture and painting. **page 176**

Vinnie Ream

(1847–1914) United States, sculptor. Ream is best known for her full sculpture of Abraham Lincoln. She was so famous in her day that she had a town named in her honor— Vinita, Oklahoma. **pages 136–137**

Gallery of Artists

 **Pierre-Auguste Renoir**

(1841–1919) France, painter. Renoir [REN•wahr] grew up in Paris, where he worked as an apprentice to a porcelain painter. He became a driving force behind the art movement called Impressionism. **page 92**

 **Bridget Riley**

(1931–) England, painter/printmaker. Riley has traveled widely but lives and works in London. She remains a leader of the Op Art movement. **page 192**

 **Diego Rivera**

(1886–1957) Mexico, muralist. Most of Rivera's murals are in Mexico City, but quite a few can be seen in the United States. He once said, "In my work, I tell the story of my nation, Mexico." **page 143**

 **Norman Rockwell**

(1894–1978) United States, painter. Rockwell is best known for his realistic illustrations of small-town life. Rockwell's big break came when he sold five color illustrations to the *Saturday Evening Post* magazine in 1916. He continued to work for the magazine until 1969. Rockwell also painted murals and illustrated books. **page 120**

 **Andre Rouillard**

page 48

 **Jessie Willcox Smith**

(1863–1935) United States, illustrator. Smith is best known for her portraits of mothers, babies, and children. She created illustrations for over forty books and for hundreds of magazine articles and covers. **page 119**

Frank Stella

(1936–) United States, painter/print-maker. In Stella's early works, he painted in an Abstract Expressionist style. However, many of his later works focus on clear geometric shapes and designs. **page 194**

Dedrick Brandes Stuber

(1878–1954) United States, painter. Stuber painted country scenes, as well as views of oceans and mountains. He preferred painting landscapes in places where it was cool and shady. **page 90**

Henry O. Tanner

(1859–1937) United States, painter. Tanner is best known for his landscapes and religious paintings. After art school, he worked as an illustrator and photographer. In 1891, he began exhibiting his works in Paris.

pages 38, 56

Wayne Thiebaud

(1920–) United States, painter. Thiebaud [TEE•boh] was born in Mesa, Arizona. He is best known for his paintings of ice cream, cakes, and hot dogs. **page 173**

Maurice Utrillo

(1883–1955) France, painter. Utrillo [oo•TREE•yoh] was encouraged by his mother to become a painter. His first paintings, mostly of Paris street scenes, were rough in texture and had dark colors. Utrillo's works later became smoother and brighter in color. **page 103**

Louis Valtat

(1869–1952) France, painter/printmaker. Valtat's early work showed the influence of Impressionism with its soft focus and colors, but by the mid-1890s he was painting with purer, stronger colors. He sometimes painted in the Fauvist style. **page 40**

Gallery of Artists

Vincent van Gogh

(1853–1890) Holland, painter. Van Gogh [van GOH] sold only one painting when he was alive, but today he is recognized as one of the most famous painters in history. He used bright colors, thick oil paint, and visible brushstrokes. Van Gogh's paintings show his strong feelings about the beauty of nature. **pages 86, 93, 130**

Victor Vasarely

(1908–1997) France, sculptor/painter/ printmaker. Vasarely [vah•zah•RAY•lee] was a founder of the Op Art movement. When he was young, Vasarely was a graphic artist who used visual tricks in his work. He also produced sculptures and worked on architectural projects. **page 193**

Diego Velázquez

(1599–1660) Spain, painter. Velázquez [vay•LAHS•kes] was the court painter for King Philip IV of Spain. One of the artist's favorite techniques was to focus intense light on his subjects and set them against dark backgrounds. **page 122**

Martha Walter

(1875–1976) United States, painter. Walter was one of the first American Impressionist painters. She often painted park and seashore scenes. **page 88**

Andy Warhol

(about 1928–1987) United States, painter. Warhol was one of the most important artists in the Pop Art movement. In many of his works, Warhol used familiar commercial images. He often repeated the images and played with their colors and sizes. **pages 50, 153**

Ralph White

(1921–) United States, painter. White received his early art training in Minnesota. After service in the United States Air Force in World War II, White continued his art education and later accepted a teaching position at the University of Texas. Much of White's art shows scenes of Texas. **page 39**

Claire Zeisler

(1903–1991) United States, fiber artist. Zeisler started out by creating traditional loom weavings, but she left the loom to make freestanding fiber sculptures. **page 184**

Francisco Zurbarán

(1598–1664) Spain, painter. Zurbarán [thuhr•bah•RAHN] is known as a major painter of the Baroque era. He often chose to paint religious subjects. His work is characterized by strong outlines, dramatic shading, and intense realism. **page 159**

Glossary

The Glossary contains important art terms and their definitions. Each word is respelled as it would be in a dictionary. When you see this mark ʹ after a syllable, pronounce that syllable with more force than the other syllables.

a add	e end	o odd	ōō pool	oi oil	ŧħ this	
ā ace	ē equal	ō open	u up	ou pout	zh vision	ə =
â care	i it	ô order	û burn	ng ring		
ä palm	ī ice	ŏŏ took	yōō fuse	th thin		

ə = { a in above / e in sicken / i in possible / o in melon / u in circus }

A

abstract art [abʹstrakt ärt] Art in which the details of real objects are simplified, distorted, or rearranged. (*See also* nonobjective.) (page 32)

analogous colors [ə•nalʹə•gəs kulʹerz] Colors that are next to each other on the color wheel. (page 39)

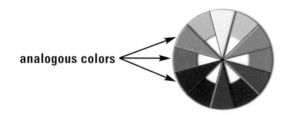

analogous colors

art prints [ärt prints] Printed copies of original artworks. (page 190)

artwork [ärtʹwûrk] A piece of art, such as a drawing, painting, or sculpture. (page 26)

assemblage [ə•semʹblij] A three-dimensional artwork made from different kinds of materials. (*See also* three-dimensional.) (page 72)

asymmetrical balance [ā•sə•meʹtri•kəl baʹləns] A type of balance achieved when two sides of an artwork are different but visually equal. (*See also* visual weight.) (page 158)

atmospheric perspective [at•məs•firʹik pər•spekʹtiv] The use of duller colors and blurred details in the middle ground and background of a painting to show distance. (page 98)

benday patterns [ben•dā′ pa′tərnz]
Patterns of lines or dots used in
comic books and other printed
materials. (page 188)

benday patterns

bust [bust] A sculpture showing
a person's head and neck and
sometimes the upper body. (page 133)

classical art [klas′i•kəl ärt] Art made
in the style of ancient Greek and
Roman artworks. (page 132)

closed form [klōzd fôrm] A sculpture
that has no openings for background
space to show through. (page 74)

complementary colors
[kom•plə•men′tər•ē kul′ərz] Pairs of
colors, such as yellow and violet, that
are opposite each other on the color
wheel. (page 40)

composition [kom•pə•zish′ən] The way
in which lines, shapes, or objects
are arranged, or put together, in an
artwork. (page 32)

computer-generated art
[kəm•pyōō′tər jen′ə•rā•təd ärt] Art
that is created with the use of a
computer. (page 198)

construction [kən•struk′shən] A
sculpture that is made of parts
joined together. (page 69)

continuous lines [kən•tin′yōō•əs līnz]
Unbroken lines. (page 170)

contour lines [kon′tŏŏr līnz] Outlines
drawn around figures or objects.
(page 29)

contrast [kon′trast] A dramatic
difference between two parts
of an artwork. (page 158)

Cubism [kyōō′biz•əm] An art style
in which parts of the subjects are
distorted or rearranged into
geometric planes, sometimes
showing different points of view
at the same time. (page 139)

diagonals [dī•ag′ə•nəlz] Slanted lines.
(page 162)

diffusion [dif•yōo′zhən] The scattering of light rays caused by water, dust, or smoke in the air. (page 99)

digital image [dij′i•təl im′ij] A picture composed entirely of electronic bits of information. (page 198)

dominant color [dom′ə•nənt kul′ər] The color that a viewer notices more than other colors in an artwork. (page 169)

emphasis [em′fə•sis] The effect created when one element is given more importance than another element in an artwork. (page 88)

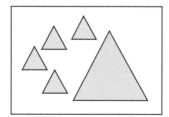

emphasis

engraving [in•grā′ving] Carving the lines of an artwork into a block or metal plate, which is covered with ink and pressed onto paper. (page 190)

environmental art [in•vī•rən•men′təl ärt] An artwork made from natural materials and placed in a natural setting; also called *earthworks art* or *land art*. (page 108)

exact symmetry [ig•zakt′ sim′ə•trē] The kind of balance created when lines, shapes, and colors are exactly the same on both sides of an artwork. (page 149)

expression [ik•spresh′ən] A look on a person's face that tells the viewer what the person is feeling. (page 122)

expressive qualities [ik•spres′iv kwäl′ə•tēz] Characteristics of art elements that make the elements affect the viewer's feelings. (page 32)

facial features [fā′shəl fē′chərz] Parts of the face, such as the eyes, nose, mouth, and ears. (page 124)

fiber art [fī′bər ärt] Artwork made from string, yarn, or cloth. (page 184)

figure [fig′yər] A human body in an artwork. (page 119)

focal point [fō′kəl point] The part of an artwork at which viewers stop and focus their attention. (page 128)

found objects [found ob′jekts] Natural or manufactured objects that are also used as art materials. (page 72)

geometric form [jē•ə•met′rik fôrm] An object that has height, width, and depth and whose sides are made up of geometric shapes. (page 78)

geometric forms

geometric shapes [jē•ə•met′rik shāps] Shapes, such as circles, triangles, and squares, that have regular outlines. (page 29)

gesture drawing [jes′chər drô′ing] A sketch created with loose arm movements. (page 28)

Golden Rectangle [gōl′dən rek′tang•gəl] A rectangle, divided into sections, that is used by artists to plan the composition of a painting. (page 164)

grid [grid] A pattern of horizontal and vertical lines like the pattern on graph paper. (page 58)

highlights [hī′līts] Areas on a surface that reflect the most light. (page 199)

horizon line [hə•rī′zən līn] A line in the distance where the land seems to meet the sky. (page 89)

horizontal axis [hôr•ə•zon′təl ak′sis] An invisible horizontal line that divides an artwork into a top half and a bottom half. (page 153)

hue [hyoo] A pure, unmixed color. (page 48)

ideal form [ī•dē′əl fôrm] Perfection of the human figure, shown in Greek and Roman art. (page 132)

installation [in•stə•lā′shən] An artwork that is placed in a specific indoor or outdoor location and that includes parts of the location in the artwork. (page 109)

intensity [in•ten′sə•tē] The brightness or dullness of a color. (page 168)

linear perspective
[li′nē•ər pər•spek′tiv] A technique in which an artist makes parallel lines come together in an artwork to create a sense of depth. (page 102)

monochromatic [mo•nə•krō•ma′tik] Relating to a color scheme that includes only one color and the tints and shades of that color. (page 38)

monochromatic

motif [mō•tēf′] A shape, design, or object that is repeated in several places in an artwork. (page 59)

movement [mōōv′mənt] The way a viewer's eyes move around an artwork. (page 93)

narrative art [nâr′ə•tiv ärt] Art that tells a story, using events and characters from history, fiction, or everyday life. (page 118)

near symmetry [nir sim′ə•trē] The kind of balance created when shapes or objects are nearly the same on both sides of an artwork. (page 149)

negative shape [ne′gə•tiv shāp] In a two-dimensional artwork, the shape of the empty areas around subjects. (page 62)

negative space [ne′gə•tiv spās] In a three-dimensional artwork, the empty space around a raised area. (page 69)

neon art [nē′on ärt] Artwork made from glass tubes filled with neon and other gases through which electricity is passed. (page 183)

neutral colors [nōō′trəl kul′ərz] Colors, such as gray and brown, that are made by mixing complementary color pigments. (*See also* complementary colors.) (page 168)

nonobjective [non•ub•jek′tiv] Relating to a kind of abstract artwork that does not show recognizable objects. (page 34)

Op Art [op ärt] A kind of abstract art that includes optical illusions. (*See also* optical illusions.) (page 192)

open form [ō′pən fôrm] A sculpture that has an opening or openings where background space shows through. (page 73)

optical illusions [op′ti•kəl i•lōō′zhənz] In two-dimensional art, effects that trick the viewer into seeing something that is not there. (page 192)

organic form [ôr•gan′ik fôrm] An object with height, width, and depth whose borders are irregular. (page 79)

organic shapes [ôr•gan′ik shāps] Shapes that have irregular borders. (page 29)

overlapping [ō•vər•lap′ing] Relating to objects that are in front of or behind other objects. (page 62)

patterns [pa′tərnz] Recognizable designs made with repeated lines, shapes, or colors. (page 58)

perspective [pər•spek′tiv] A technique used to create a feeling of depth, or distance, in a painting. (page 92)

photomontage [fō•tō•mon′•täzh′] An artwork made up of photographs. (page 44)

photorealistic [fō•tō•rē•ə•lis′tik] Relating to a kind of painting that is so detailed that it might be mistaken for a photograph. (page 42)

pigment [pig′mənt] A colored powder commonly mixed with liquid to make paint. (page 182)

placement [plās′mənt] The technique of placing objects higher in a painting or drawing to show depth or distance. (page 92)

placement

point of view [point əv vyo͞o] The position from which an artist looks at a subject while creating an artwork. (page 88)

Pop Art [pop ärt] A kind of art that often features common objects, letters, and numbers in a style similar to the art in advertisements and comic strips. (page 50)

portrait [pôr′trət] An artwork whose subject is a person. (page 122)

pose [pōz] The body position a model holds while an artist sketches, paints, or sculpts his or her portrait. (page 118)

positive shape [pä′zə•tiv shāp] In a two-dimensional artwork, the shape of subjects that have empty areas around them. (page 62)

positive space [pä′zə•tiv spās] In a three-dimensional artwork, the space occupied by a raised area. (page 69)

profile [prō′fīl] A side view of a
subject. (page 140)

proportion [prə•pôr′shən] A sense
that objects are the correct size in
comparison with one another.
(page 92)

quadrant pattern [kwäd′rənt pa′tərn] A
four-part pattern with four ninety-
degree angles. (page 153)

quadrant patterns

radial balance [rā′dē•əl ba′ləns] The
kind of balance created when the
parts of an artwork extend from its
center like the spokes of a wheel.
(page 154)

representational [rep•ri•zen•tā′shən•əl]
Relating to a kind of art in which
subjects look realistic. (page 42)

rhythm [ri′thəm] The visual beat
created by the regular repetition of
elements in an artwork. (page 178)

saturation [sa•chə•rā′shən] The
brightness of a color. Pure, unmixed
colors have high saturation. (page 48)

self-portrait [self•pôr′trət] An artwork
in which the artist is the subject.
(page 128)

sequential [sē•kwen′shəl] Relating to
the arrangement of the parts of an
artwork in a series of steps.
(page 163)

shading [shād′•ing] The use of value
to create shadows on objects in flat
artworks. (page 159)

soft sculpture [sôft skulp′chər] A three-
dimensional artwork made of soft
materials such as canvas or foam
rubber. (page 179)

space [spās] The area between, around,
or within objects. (page 89)

still life [stil līf] An artwork that shows
a group of objects arranged in a
composition. (page 60)

Surrealism [sə•rē′ə•li•zəm] A type of
art that features confusing and
dreamlike images. (page 48)

symbol [sim′bəl] A word, picture, or object that stands for, or represents, something else. (page 138)

symbol

symmetrical balance

[sə•me′tri•kəl ba′ləns] The kind of balance created when an equal number of similar shapes or objects are placed on each side of an artwork. (page 148)

tactile texture [tak′təl teks′chər] The way the surface of a real object feels when you touch it. (page 129)

tessellation [tes•ə•lā′shən] A pattern of shapes that fit together without overlapping and without having empty spaces between them. (page 63)

three-dimensional [thrē•də•men′shə•nəl] Having height, width, and depth. (page 68)

two-dimensional [tōō•də•men′shə•nəl] Having height and width. (page 68)

unity [yōō′nə•tē] The sense that an artwork is complete and that its parts work together as a whole. (page 152)

value [val′yōō] The lightness or darkness of a color. (page 38)

vanishing point [van′ish•ing point] The point on the horizon line where parallel lines seem to meet and disappear. (page 104)

variety [və•rī′ə•tē] The interesting effect created when one element is different from other elements in an artwork. (page 178)

vertical axis [vər′ti•kəl ak′sis] An invisible vertical line through the center of an artwork. (page 148)

visual texture [vizh′ōō•əl teks′chər] Drawn or painted texture that looks like real texture. (page 129)

visual weight [vizh′ōō•əl wāt] The importance given to objects or shapes by their size, color, or placement in an artwork. (page 148)

Art History
Time Line

PREHISTORIC **3,000** B.C. **ANCIENT** **500** B.C. **CLASSICAL** A.D. **476**

Unknown Artist
The Red Horse and the Bull

Unknown Artist
Male Face

Unknown Artist
Chariot of Apollo

ROMANTICISM **1800** **REALISM** **1870** **IMPRESSIONISM**

Jennie Augusta Brownscombe
Dolley Madison's Ball

Winslow Homer
Kissing the Moon

Berthe Morisot
Butterfly Hunt

FAUVISM **1900** **CUBISM** **1920** **HARLEM RENAISSANCE**

Henri Matisse
Interior with Egyptian Curtain

Pablo Picasso
L'Italienne

Romare Bearden
New Orleans: Ragging Home

MEDIEVAL **1453** RENAISSANCE **1600** BAROQUE/ROCOCO

Unknown Artist
Rose Window,
Notre Dame Cathedral

Michelangelo
David (detail)

Diego Velázquez
Juan de Pareja

POST-
IMPRESSIONISM POINTILLISM **1890** EXPRESSIONISM

Vincent van Gogh
Café Terrace on the Place du Forum

Georges Seurat
Bathers at Asnières

Franz Marc
Monkey Frieze

SURREALISM **1945** ABSTRACT
EXPRESSIONISM **1960** POP ART

Salvador Dalí
Telephone-Homard

Jackson Pollock
Convergence

Andy Warhol
Six Self-Portraits

Index of
Artists and Artworks

Index

Index

Index

Acknowledgments

Acknowledgments

109 Karl Ciesluk/Superstock; 110 (l) Courtesy of the Artist and Galerie Lelong, New York; (r) Julian Calder/Corbis; 113 © 2006 Artists Right Society (ARS) New York, NY/ Musee d'Orsay, Paris/Lauros-Giraudon, Paris/Superstock.

Unit 4

114 Smithsonian American Art Museum, Washington, DC/Art Resource, NY; 115 (b) Eduardo Chavez/Courtesy of Bruce Currie/Woodstock Artists Association; 116 (b) Dolly Madison's Ball by Jennie Augusta Brownscombe, Courtesy of The Louise & Alan Sellars Collection of Art by American Women, Indianapolis, IN. 118 Architect of the Capitol, neg. 70611; 119 (t) Blue Lantern Studio/Corbis; 120 Corbis; 122 Metropolitan Museum of Art, New York/Bridgeman Art Library; 123 (t) Collection of the Lowe Art Museum, University of Miami. Museum purchase through the funds from Friends of Art and public subscription, 82.0024/Licensed by VAGA, New York, NY, (b) Christie's Images/Superstock; 124 (b) Giraudon/Art Resource, NY; 126 Corbis; 127 (tl) Corbis; (br) Do Wah Diddy; 128 Private Collection/GG Kopilak/Superstock; 129 Banco de Mexico Trust/Digital Image/The Museum of Modern Art/Licensed by SCALA/Art Resource, NY; 130 Art Resource, NY; 132 Superstock; 133 Hermitage Museum, St. Petersburg, Russia/Leonid Bogdanov/Superstock; 134 (l) Kimbell Art Museum, Fort Worth, TX; (r) Kimbell Art Museum, Fort Worth, TX; 136 (tr) Smithsonian American Art Museum, Washington, DC/Art Resource, NY; (bl) Corbis; 137 (bl) Kelly-Mooney Photography/Corbis; 137 (tr) Architect of the Capitol, neg. 70043; 138 Reunion des Musees Nationaux/Art Resource, NY; 139 Russisches Museum, St. Petersburg/Superstock; 140 Brianna/Westbrook Elementary School, West Islip, NY; 143 Christie's Images/Corbis;

Unit 5

144 Francis G. Mayer/Corbis; 145 (b) Bettmann/Corbis; 146 Private Collection/Patricia Schwimmer/Superstock; 148 Dave Bartruff/Corbis; 149 Nimatallah/Art Resource, NY; 150 © 2006 Artists Right Society (ARS) New York, NY/Digital Image © The Museum of Modern Art/Licensed by SCALA/Art Resource, NY; 152 The Pierpont Morgan Library/Art Resource, NY; 153 © 2006 The Andy Warhol Foundation for the Visual Arts /© 2006 Artists Right Society (ARS) New York, NY/Art Resource, NY; 154 (bl) © Erich Lessing/Art Resource, NY; (br) Peter Richards/Childs Elementary School; 156 Kunsthistorisches Museum, Vienna, Austria/The Bridgeman Art Library; 157 (bl) Erich Lessing/Art Resource, NY; (tr) Mark L. Stephenson/Corbis; 158 Francis G. Mayer/Corbis; 159 Erich Lessing/Art Resource, NY; 160 Musee d'Orsay, Paris/ET Archive, London/Superstock; 162 © Erich Lessing/Art Resource, NY; 163 David David Gallery, Philadelphia/Superstock; 164 The Huntington Library, Art Collections, and Botanical Gardens, San Marino, California/Superstock; 166 (t) Alison Wright/Corbis; 167 (b) Index Stock Imagery; (tr) Kevin Schafer/Corbis; 168 Weinberg Collection, Zurich/Lauros-Giraudon, Paris/Superstock; 169 Freshman Brown/Superstock; 173 Spencer Museum of Art, The University of Kansas/Gift of Ralph T. Coe in memory of Helen F. Spencer/Licensed by VAGA, New York, NY.

Unit 6

174 Teresa Rishel/Chihuly Studio; 175 AP/Wide World Photos; 176 Licensed by VAGA, New York, NY/Kate Ganz USA Ltd.; 178 © 2006 Artists Right Society (ARS) New York, NY/The Museum of Contemporary Art, Los Angeles, CA. Gift of Mr. and Mrs. Arnold Glimcher; 179 Art Gallery of Ontario, Toronto, Canada/Bridgeman Art Library; 180 Geoffrey Clements/Corbis; 182 Tate Gallery, London/Art Resource, NY; 183 Joseph Sohm/Visions of America, LLC/PictureQuest; 184 The Metropolitan Museum of Art, Gift of Peter Florsheim, Thomas W. Florsheim, and Joan Florsheim-Binkley, 1987 (1987.371) Photograph (c) 1995, The Metropolitan Museum of Art; 186 (t) Jesús Moroles; (b) Evan Agostini/Jesús Moroles; 187 (b) Jesús Moroles; 187 GoodShoot/Superstock; 188 Albright-Knox Art Gallery, Buffalo, New York, Edmond Hayes and Charles Clifton Funds; 189 David Lees, Licensed by VAGA, New York, NY/Corbis; 190 © 2006 Artists Right Society (ARS) New York, NY/Morgan Art Foundation Limited/Art Resource, NY; 192 Digital Image/The Museum of Modern Art/Licensed by SCALA/Art Resource, NY; 193 © 2006 Artists Right Society (ARS) New York, NY/Erich Lessing/Art Resource, NY; 194 Frank Stella/© 2006 Artists Right Society (ARS) New York, NY/Art Resource, NY; 196 (t) Bill Ross/Corbis; (b) Stocktrek/Corbis; 197 (b) Alamy Images; (t) Bill Ross/Corbis; 198 (br) Robert Rak; (tl), (cl), (bl) Marlin Studios; 199 Ronald Davis; 200 Courtesy of the Artist; 203 © 2006 Artists Right society (ARS) New York, NY/Art Resource, NY;

Backmatter

Artist Gallery

Anguissola: The Bridgeman Art Library; Archimboldo: The Granger Collection; Audubon: Bettmann/Corbis; Bearden: Chester Higgins, Jr.; Bernini: Ashmolean Museum, Oxford, UK/Bridgeman Art Library; Botticelli: Scala/Art Resource, NY; Brewster: Susan McClatchy; Brownscombe: Wayne County (PA) Historical Society; Calder: Jean Gaumy/Magnum Photos; Cassatt: The Metropolitan Museum of Art, Bequest of Edith H. Proskauer, 1975; Cezanne: Erich Lessing/Art Resource, NY; Chihuly: AP/Wide World Photos; Ciesluk: Karl Ciesluk; da Vinci: Mary Evans Picture Library; Degas: Giraudon/Art Resource, NY; Dulaunay: Painting by Metzinger/© 2006 Artists Rights Society (ARS), NY/Bettmann/Corbis; Dwight: AP/Wide World Photos; Escher's "Selfportrait" © 2003 Cordon Art B.V. - Baarn - Holland. All rights reserved; Fish: Stewart & Stewart; Freshman Brown: Superstock; Giambologna: Louvre, Paris, France/Lauros/Giraudon/Bridgeman Art Library; Glen: Robert Glen Gallery; Goldsworthy: Philippe Caron/Corbis; Graves: Steven Sloman/Nancy Graves Foundation; Groff: Painter, www.larrygroff.com/John Lawrence Groff; Hanson: Estate of Duane Hanson/Licensed by VAGA, New York, NY/Duane Hanson Estate; Homer: Bettmann/Corbis; Hopper: National Portrait Gallery, Smithsonian Institution/Art Resource, NY; Indiana: Stephen O. Muskie; Johns: Christopher Felver/Corbis; Kahlo: Bettmann/Corbis; Kandinsky: Roger Viollet/Getty Images; Kapoor: Christopher Felver/Corbis; Klee: Hulton Archive/Getty Images; Kopilak: GG Kopilak; Lichtenstein: Christopher Felver/Corbis; Magafan: Eduardo